MAYA

Text by
PIERRE IVANOFF

Foreword
MIGUEL ANGEL ASTURIAS

MONUMENTS OF CIVILIZATION

CASSELL · LONDON

For permission to reprint extensive excerpts from the major Mayan sacred-historical texts, we gratefully acknowledge the following:

From *The Annals of The Cakchiquels*, translated by Adrian Recinos and Delia Goetz. Copyright 1953 by the University of Oklahoma Press.

From *Popol Vuh: The Sacred Book of the Ancient Quiché Maya*, English version by Delia Goetz and Sylvanus G. Morley, from the Spanish translation by Adrian Recinos. Copyright 1950 by the University of Oklahoma Press.

From *The Book of Chilam Balam of Chumayel*, by Ralph L. Roys. Courtesy of Carnegie Institution, Washington, D.C. Publication No. 438. 1933.

Other quoted material is acknowledged at its point of use.

In addition, for providing particular photographs, special thanks go to the following: Bernard LeMoniet and André Falque; Enrique F. Torrijos for the photos on pages 22 and 34; Armando S. Portugal for the photos on pages, 2, 61, 64, 159, 172–73; Hans Ritter for the photos on pages 79, 82–4; and the American Museum of Madrid for the photo on page 89.

CASSELL & COMPANY LTD

an imprint of
Cassell & Collier Macmillan Publishers Ltd
35 Red Lion Square, London WC1R 4SG
and at Sydney, Auckland, Toronto, Johannesburg

and an affiliate of The Macmillan Company Inc., New York

English translation copyright © 1973 by Mondadori,
Milano-Kodansha, Tokyo; originally published in
Italian under the title *Grandi Monumenti: CITTÀ MAYA*
copyright © 1970 by Mondadori, Milano-Kodansha,
Tokyo; copyright © 1970 by Kodansha Ltd., Tokyo,
for the illustrations; copyright © 1970 by Mondadori,
Milano-Kodansha, Tokyo for the text.

First published in Great Britain 1975

ISBN: 0 304 29434 9

Printed and bound in Italy by Mondadori, Verona

Editorial Director
GIULIANA NANNICINI
American Editorial Supervisor
JOHN BOWMAN

Frontispiece:
Palenque: Temple of the Inscriptions. This view of the interior of the burial crypt shows the carved stone that covers the sarcophagus.

CONTENTS

FOREWORD

Oh pyramids, temples, and monuments, witnesses of thousands of years of splendor, speak the language of the enigma! Where should one begin if your presence is magical? Answer, if you can, what was the fate of the Maya! The grass has grown and is silent. Answer if you can, what was the fate of all the sea captains that have come here? The grass has grown and is silent. Answer, if you can, what has become of the one we invoke in these forests: "Our Father, who are not on a bed of roses, blessed be the soles of thy feet, and may, Cuauhtémoc, thy will of lava be done!"

The grass has grown and is silent. The voyage has no return. No one ever returned from the green world where among deer and blue peacocks there arose ceremonial, cosmic, and frozen cities — the challenge of builder-peoples, of men of other suns, of men that live as if the centuries had not gone by; a race counting its days like diamonds and trusting in its gods, in its rites of smoke and dreams, in its calendar stones, in the music of words, in its wisdom, in everything that five centuries of devastation, exploitation, and oblivion have never been able to annihilate completely! What is left of those cultures, their system of time, their divinities, their music, their songs, their dances, their manner of tilling the soil? Much is left — and not only has it withstood the passing of five hundred years, it is born anew by inspiring such powerful artistic forms as the great mural paintings of Mexico and the skyscraper architecture of New York.

The Mayan gods descend the steps of the great stairways, steps covered with astronomical inscriptions at Copán; then they disappear, abstract and marvelous, transmuted into jaguars of obsidian. It was these civilizing gods that taught the inhabitants of the plateaus of Guatemala (who can say in which millennium?) to cultivate maize, exactly as it is sown and reaped today, the white and yellow maize with which, according to the indigenous scripture, the first human beings were made; together with the maize they cultivated the other foods and elements of life: beans, pumpkins, cocoa, tobacco, sweet potatoes, yuccas, tubers, red bell peppers, copal, incense, rubber, red pine, and cotton, all soaked with the humidity of the terrain. And what of the animals that filled this legendary world: jaguars, pumas, tapirs, armadillos, deer, coyotes, boar, lizards, bats, snakes, foxes, monkeys, rabbits, tortoises, eagles, crows, owls, parrots, turkeys, fireflies, and worms.

Amidst these tropical wildernesses are the remains of mysterious, fascinating cities of which modern man knows very little or nothing. The admiration one feels in front of these monuments is infinite — but is less than the astonishment generated by the inexplicable: that in the midst of these flooded lands, in the humidity and in the heat, wizard architects threw tons of stone into flying edifices — and sculptors who thought they were modeling clouds restored to them their heaviness through massive forms in bas-relief and high-relief, reproduced from the surrounding flora and fauna.

Statuary of joy, of joy and of death, different by virtue of its austere grace from all other sculptures and arts of antiquity, particularly from the plastic arts of Asia, in which so many observers feel they can find kinships or similarities. Nothing could be more mistaken, further from the truth. The Mayan plastic arts are oceans and continents away from the equivocal, lascivious, sexual world of paunchy Buddhas and slimy gods. "Not the slightest trace of all this honied, ectoplastic Hindu sexuality," wrote Aldous Huxley, "is to be found in the art of the Maya. Here the feminine form is never seen. And the masculine body, when revealing itself in its hieratical ornaments, is always obligatorily male. It never takes on the hermaphroditic attributes that distinguish, in Hindu art, gods and saviors." And then Huxley goes on to say: "Hindu artists display their skill in accentuating sexual attributes, making use of plastic symbols with the aim of achieving an esthetic emotion accompanied by the immediate contact of flesh with flesh, in pictorial, sculptural, and even architectural forms. But the Maya never used their singular artistic abilities in this way. Their decorative forms are devoid of sensuality, and nearly always avoid direct representation of erotic scenes, or of those that can be called erotically significant personages. In Mayan art, sex does not exist."

As far as ornamentation is concerned, Huxley adds: "Their sacred personages never use tight fitting or curved mitres, as the Hindus do. The ornaments on their heads are pure geometrical abstractions, like the neat cones and cylinders worn by the people in the frescoes of Piero della Francesca. At times their hairdos consist of fantastic combinations of symbolic and decorative motifs. They are representations of the feather tiaras used by high-ranking personalities. These feather halos, decorations of cubist mathematical designs, become naturalistic or austerely abstract in their formal distribution. Among the most exorbitant Mayan ornamental combinations appear hieroglyphics: compared to these the fantasies of Gothic decorations seem pedestrian. But however rich and bizarre they may be, these flights of the creative imagination are always rigidly disciplined, subjected to the control of a highly severe intellectual order."

All this can easily be ascertained by observing Mayan art. The splendid illustrations making up this book attest to the power of that civilization in which the artists, at the moment of creation, miraculously transcended their environment, isolating themselves from the sensual world surrounding them: a warm, perfumed world, in perennial metamorphosis, among fragrant flowers, balsams and mosses, more propitious to voluptuous delectation than to the rigor of mental disciplines. These marvelous monuments attest not only to the artistic progress of those peoples, but also to the level they attained in everything connected to philosophical thought, education, and creative ability. Great sculptors, painters, and architects had to be familiar, among other things, with the language of symbols in order to achieve fully the ideal of the art they characterized as "the apotheosis of every-thing that is human and humanization of everything divine." Their essential task was to elevate humanity to mathematical and astral heights and to assume the divine in order to deify whatever pertained to man.

The vestiges of these remote cultures live on in texts, murals, carved stone, and ceramics, which we seek to approach through a scientific investigation. Luckily we can study everything that remains of them in the living styles, beliefs, and customs of indigenous peoples who have not disappeared. It is indispensable to stress this point. These staggering Mayan edifices come to us from cultures and peoples that are still living — though they no longer build nor sculpt. The most beautiful ceramics still attest to the artistic abilities of their hands. The people of the Yucatán and regions of Guatemala no longer paint great frescoes, but the fabrics they offer are as good as paintings. Their symbolic colors, and the whole range of their protecting signs in small vegetal, animal, and cosmic figures closely resemble the designs of the Mayan codes. These descendants no longer celebrate, as their ancestors once did, in temples and public squares surrounded by stelae and offering stones, but rather in churches, in front of blood-spattered images of Christ.

The Mayan spirit still lives among the peoples currently living in the same territories — as with the Lacandón Indians, still absolutely primitive, who live like their ancestors, self-sufficient, producing every-thing they consume: their clothes and their hunting and fishing equip-ment. Even the communities that are closest to our own culture are based on a type of existence that closely follows the historical forms of the primitive Maya: their beliefs and religious cults, their farming and handicraft methods, and their birth, marriage, and death customs. It is precisely this survival of Mayan influences that makes the monu-ments of their ceremonial centers — pyramids, palaces, temples, stairways, ball courts, and great stelae (whose styles of carving are now converted into precious embroidery) — take on a significance different from the remains of other noble civilizations. The Mayan sites are not relics, dead materials, extraneous to all historical horizons. On the contrary, the moment they are discovered by archaeologists they are besieged not only by artists, especially sculptors, but also by the learned in human sciences who analyze them in the light of their own knowledge of the customs of the surviving indigenous groups.

Our knowledge of the ball game the Maya played would be frag-mentary if we could not survey the ball courts on which the games were played. And if we speak theoretically of the pyramids, of their rising out of the ground to touch the heavens with linear wings, or of the buoyancy of their monumental masses, a sight of them as they really are provides us with the most exhaustive confirmation. The grandeur of the facades, the enormity of the stucco masks, and the peaks of the pyramids vibrate with an upward motion that gives a sensation of liberty, joy, and festivity. The Mayan language also vibrates — still spoken by a million and a half Indian descendants. It is precisely for this reason that this great culture, alive in its roots, must be included in the current dialogue of cultures — with its message of beauty, its human dimension, and its perennial rebirth. Fearful cataclysms and wars of conquest have sought to annihilate its history, its traditions, its customs, its religion, its life. Yet this culture has survived the vicissitudes of the centuries and now extends its horizons with new esthetic evaluations and the application of architectural methods that are surprisingly modern. Its most ancient texts incite us to study original concepts of the universe, survival in the world beyond, the destiny of man, the function of thought, and the development of science and the arts.

Follow the magic that leads from page to page in this collection of images of the inestimable treasures of the Mayan culture. The author, Pierre Ivanoff, who himself has made a pilgrimage, is the guide through the depths of the forest, to the prodigious cities that fascinate us, stopping off at Palenque, city of marvelous stuccoes, at Copán, the city of astronomies, at Quiriguá, city of the stelae of flowering stone, and at Yaxchilán, Dos Pozos, and many other ceremonial centers. Not to mention Tikal, the city of voices, where, according to the Indians, strange voices are heard.

Miguel Angel Asturias
(Nobel Prize for Literature 1967)

INTRODUCTION

Forgotten and all but lost for many hundreds of years in the forests and scrub growth of Central America, the remains of literally thousands of once-grand structures eloquently illustrate one of the most stimulating chapters in the history of mankind. The physical characteristics alone of these abandoned Mayan sites — the temple-pyramids that reach as high as 224 feet, the magnificent stone stelae and altars, the provocative bas-relief carvings, the polychrome ceramics, the mysterious hieroglyphic signs carved on the monuments — all testify to the high level of civilization reached by their creators.

But beyond such attainments, the very presence of these "ghost cities" in the forest that extends from the Guatemalan territory of Petén into Honduras and northward into Mexico (see the map, page 14) is in itself something of an enigma. This region is hot and humid for the most part, difficult to penetrate because of thick vegetation and generally hostile to man's domesticating activities. So it is that the civilization it once sustained continues to baffle the most capable specialists and to attract the most curious amateurs.

The first truly modern responses to the Mayan civilization were made by the celebrated nineteenth-century American traveler, John Lloyd Stephens, and his English companion, the artist Frederick Catherwood, who rediscovered Copán, still one of the most illustrious sites, in November 1839. A few months later, after visiting a second site farther north, Palenque, Stephens was already setting forth the hypothesis that the area between the two centers had been inhabited by people who shared the same culture. He based his theory principally on the similarities in hieroglyphic inscriptions found in each area.

The hopes of learning more about this elusive civilization were rekindled in the 1860s when a French scholar-monk, Abbé Brasseur de Bourbourg, discovered an old manuscript, the *Relación de las cosas de Yucatán* ("Account of Things in the Yucatán") in the Royal Library of Madrid, Spain. This was a work, written shortly after the Spanish conquest of Mexico, by Father Diego de Landa, the first Catholic Bishop of Mérida, the Spaniards' capital city in the Yucatán. His account was based on his contacts with sixteenth-century Indians of the Yucatán and included ethnographic information (often based on oral traditions) of inestimable value. It also contained actual drawings of the hieroglyphic writing used by the descendants of the classical Maya. Along with other zealous Christians of that time, Landa had participated in burning most of the precious painted manuscripts written in the hieroglyphic language, the sacred and traditional texts of the Maya and thus obstacles to their conversion. It is one of the minor ironies of history that this same Bishop de Landa wrote an account that, despite various errors and limitations, remains one of the fundamental sources of our knowledge on the ancient Maya civilization.

The discovery of Bishop de Landa's manuscript caused a great deal of interest in Europe and America, because the hieroglyphic characters reproduced in it were similar to those recorded by Stephens and subsequent explorers at Central American sites. This was evidence of a cultural relationship between the early builders of Guatemala and the sixteenth-century Indians inhabiting the Yucatán peninsula, a relationship made more interesting by an affinity of architectural characteristics between the crumbling edifices of the south and the abandoned monuments of Mexico.

In the last two decades of the nineteenth century, many universities and institutions, particularly in the United States, sponsored excavations in Central America, launching a scientific investigation into the Mayan world. The term "Maya," which had designated until then a large portion of the Yucatán Indians, was adapted as the name of the whole civilization. (During the course of their history, these Indians had established a league known as the "Mayapán." Other than that, it is not known what they called themselves as a people.)

After a century of study, scholars have unraveled many facts and have proposed many theories concerning the culture of the Mayan people — both through on-site archaeological observations and through an examination of relevant texts. (In addition to Bishop de Landa's manuscript, three original Mayan codices have been discovered, while other indigenous documents, such as the *Books of Chilam Balam*, the *Popol Vuh*, and the *Annals of the Cakchiquels*, have provided useful data.) And although much information remains to be collected and analyzed, a few generalizations can be made about the Maya.

The "classical" Maya civilization emerged about the third century A.D. and ended about the tenth century. Evidence spanning this length of time has been found both in the northern and southern sites, although there is a preponderance of early remains in the Petén region of Guatemala. For this reason, it has been proposed that the Mayan civilization culture originated in Petén, was divided politically into independent city-states, and gradually spread north into the Yucatán with waves of emigrants from the fifth century on. (The only site in the Yucatán that has revealed evidence of the classical Maya before the fifth century is that of Dzibilchaltún, the latest to be excavated.)

Perhaps the major characteristic of the Mayan people that has emerged was their obsession with the passage of time. They were prodigious astronomers, noting the movements of Venus and predicting eclipses of the sun and moon, and they were expert in the manipulation of highly complex calendars. In fact, they invented a sun calendar more precise than the Gregorian calendar used today — although they had no means of measuring small segments of time, such as hours, minutes, and seconds, because they never invented even a sandglass or a water clock.

With such a preoccupation with time, the Mayans became fine mathematicians. They conceived the notion of zero, and their system of numerical position enabled them to calculate in numbers exceeding one million. (One hieroglyphic inscription on a Mayan monument, if taken literally, refers to a date four hundred million years ago.) On the other hand, there is no evidence to indicate that they used multiplication, division, fractions, or weights and measures.

Many of the tall Mayan pyramids topped with temples appear to have been built for astronomical purposes, while others seem to have been centers of religious activity. The Mayan conception of divinities was also related to time, with particular calendar days ascribed to particular deities. Any detailed account of religious beliefs, hierarchy, or political structure is difficult, however, because most of the hieroglyphs that have been translated pertain to calculations of time and related events. The Mayan forms of government were probably theocratic and hereditary, but there is no definitive proof of this.

The Mayans were accomplished technicians in some ways. They knew how to make cement and built immense structures using it as mortar. They also built roads, but for processions only, as they never discovered the wheel. They developed a corbel vault as an arch, but its strength was dependent on cement instead of its technical design. They were marvelous sculptors, but the only tools they seem to have used were of polished stone, of a type belonging to the Neolithic Age. Their methods of agriculture were also primitive; they cultivated maize and many other crops, but in the preparation of their fields they never advanced beyond chopping down trees with axes of polished stone and burning over the stumps and stubble.

About the beginning of the tenth century, the Maya seem to have abruptly ceased their architectural and sculptural activities. The sites in the northern region were apparently overtaken by Toltec invaders from central Mexico, who both borrowed some customs from the Maya and lent them some of their own — including warfare and human sacrifice. In the centuries that followed, these new people constructed buildings in the Yucatán with a mixture of Toltec and Mayan elements, but the sites in Guatemala and the Chiapas region of Mexico were never occupied again. What happened to bring about such a drastic end to the classic Mayan civilization is one of the major disputes and concerns of modern students of the subject.

This book reflects such developments with its division into two parts — the classical Mayan sites, which are concentrated in the southern regions, and the post-classical sites, which are in the Yucatán. Some secondary sites, as well as the principal Mayan centers, are presented, because occasionally modest remains best express the evolution of certain aspects of Mayan culture. Each site in this work can be considered one of the many pieces that make up the gigantic Mayan mosaic. Along with the sculptures and various other works of art illustrated here, and the excerpts from certain Mayan texts, these pieces combine to help the reader grasp the role of the Mayan adventure in the larger history of mankind.

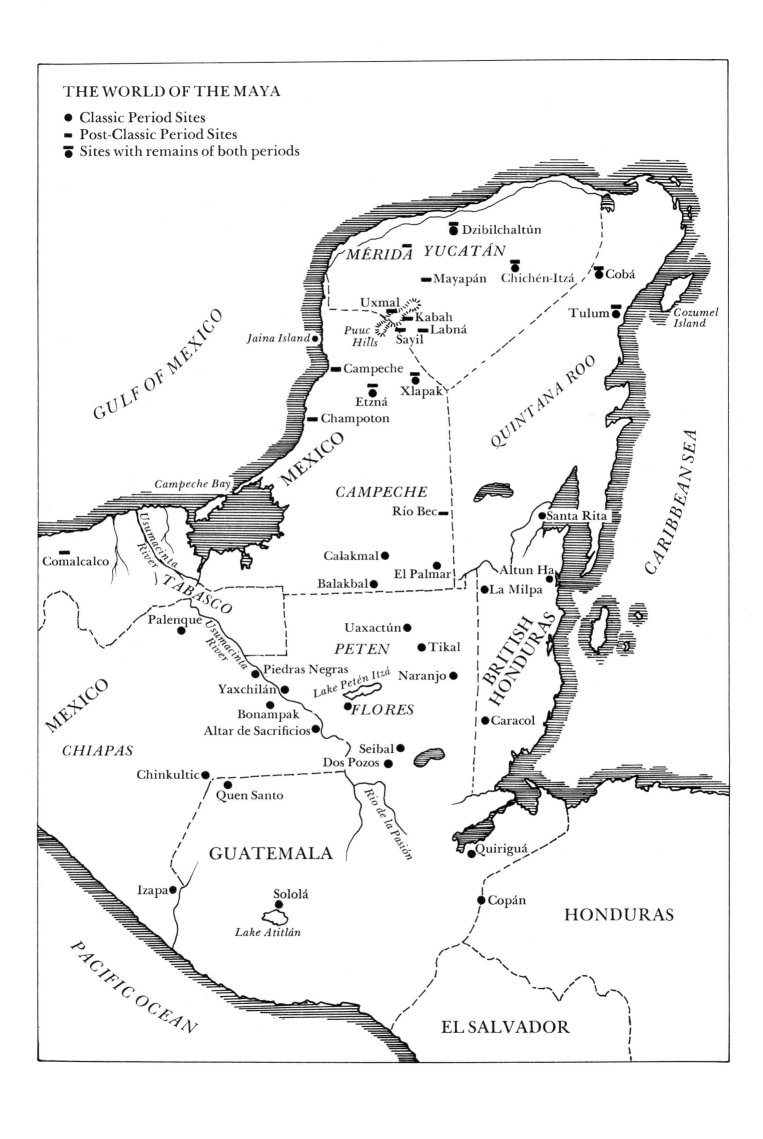

THE WORLD OF THE MAYA

● Classic Period Sites
▬ Post-Classic Period Sites
⊤ Sites with remains of both periods

GULF OF MEXICO

MÉRIDA *YUCATÁN*

▬ Dzibilchaltún

▬ Mayapán Chichén-Itzá ⊤ Cobá

Uxmal

Jaina Island ● Kabah
▬ Labná
Puuc Sayil
Hills

▬ Campeche

Etzná ● ▬ Xlapak

▬ Champoton

MEXICO

Campeche Bay

CAMPECHE

Río Bec ▬

Santa Rita ●

▬ Comalcalco Calakmal ●
El Palmar ●
Balakbal ● Altun Ha ●
La Milpa ●

TABASCO

Palenque ●

Usumacinta River

PETEN

Uaxactún ●

Tikal ●

Piedras Negras ●

Lake Petén Itzá

Naranjo ●

BRITISH HONDURAS

Yaxchilán ●

FLORES

Bonampak ●
Altar de Sacrificios ●

Seibal ●
Dos Pozos ●

Caracol ●

MEXICO

CHIAPAS

Chinkultic ●

Quen Santo ●

Río de la Pasión

GUATEMALA

Izapa ●

Sololá ●

Quiriguá ●

Copán ●

HONDURAS

Lake Atitlán

PACIFIC OCEAN

EL SALVADOR

QUINTANA ROO

Tulum ⊤ *Cozumel Island*

CARIBBEAN SEA

THE CLASSIC PERIOD

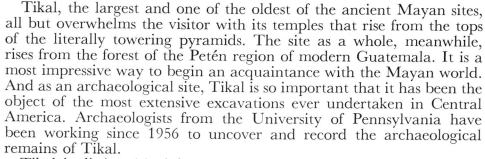

TIKAL

Tikal, the largest and one of the oldest of the ancient Mayan sites, all but overwhelms the visitor with its temples that rise from the tops of the literally towering pyramids. The site as a whole, meanwhile, rises from the forest of the Petén region of modern Guatemala. It is a most impressive way to begin an acquaintance with the Mayan world. And as an archaeological site, Tikal is so important that it has been the object of the most extensive excavations ever undertaken in Central America. Archaeologists from the University of Pennsylvania have been working since 1956 to uncover and record the archaeological remains of Tikal.

Tikal is distinguished from other Mayan sites by the height of its pyramids, the size and quantity of its constructions, and the fact that it includes the most ancient definitive date linked to a Mayan site: the year A.D. 292, inscribed in the stone of Stele 29. (Other evidence, which we shall peruse shortly, and which includes maize pollen, indicates that people — not necessarily Mayan, of course — were living in this area by at least 600 B.C.) Scattered throughout the area of some six square miles (the total "city" was probably more like twenty-five square miles) are some 3,000 known constructions. As a group they represent all the major features of a Mayan site: flat-topped step pyramids that support temples decorated with tiled pediments, known as "roof combs"; realistic bas-reliefs; jutting corbeled vaults; areas for ball games; steam baths; edifices built around large open public squares; tombs that conceal polychrome ceramics; and stelae, altars, and monoliths sculpted with extraordinary personages surrounded by hieroglyphic inscriptions.

The central buildings in Mayan cities were apparently used for religious, ceremonial functions and were also used as markets. And while the idea of a "city" implies a concentration of individuals living in close proximity, the arrangement of many of the Mayan sites has led scholars to doubt that they were really urban settlements. It is possible, of course, that a small elite did live there, while the rest of the Mayas visited the centers only for specific purposes. As John Lloyd Stephens, the first American to visit and record his impressions of the Mayan World, supposed in the nineteenth century: "The architectural complexes of the Mayan cities were most likely made up of a succession of gigantic altars, built by an entire population subject to a tiny theocratic minority, which was demanding and tyrannical."

While the Mayan architect had no concern for interior space, nor any preoccupation with a city-wide vision of architecture, the achievement of his works is outstanding. A reading of the map of Tikal gives an idea of the structural anarchy found in many Mayan cities — where no "golden rule" of town planning existed. A comparison of the sites reveals that it is impossible to discern any general order of distribution, orientation, or disposition of the structures. Each architectural grouping is made up of a disordered mass of structures, and roads are rare.

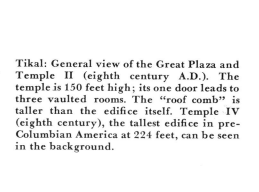

Tikal: General view of the Great Plaza and Temple II (eighth century A.D.). The temple is 150 feet high; its one door leads to three vaulted rooms. The "roof comb" is taller than the edifice itself. Temple IV (eighth century), the tallest edifice in pre-Columbian America at 224 feet, can be seen in the background.

Only the central plaza of Tikal, situated between the Northern Acropolis and the Central Acropolis, seems to present monuments in well-defined positions. Called the Great Plaza, this area appears to have been used for essentially ceremonial and religious purposes. Almost all of the city's stelae (discussed in a later section) are enclosed in this plaza, which is bounded on the east by Temple I and on the west by Temple II.

The Central Acropolis, more than five acres large, consists of five courtyards set on different levels surrounded by forty-five edifices one or more stories high containing hundreds of rooms. Tradition has named these structures "palaces," but perhaps a bit arbitrarily. Whether they were ever residences, or were perhaps simple storerooms for storing sacred victuals, is not known. It is possible that the narrow, dark rooms served as living cells for priests or as administrative offices.

Among the three thousand structures in the center of Tikal, a hundred small constructions stand out. These structures, built in the ninth century, appear in groups of four or five, always constructed on top of artificial mounds. In the immediate vicinity of each of these little "islands," probably inhabited by members of the same family, there are vestiges of numerous storerooms made of stone covered with stucco, and once covered with thatch roofs. In domestic architecture such as this, a great variety in building composition has been found, which suggests some form of economic and social differences among the inhabitants.

The density of structures at Tikal is considerable; yet in all this mass of constructions no area was reserved for agriculture to support a permanently settled population. Taking into account the archaic agricultural system of the time, it has been calculated that in order to feed the population of Tikal (were it fully occupied) a land area of about 200 square miles would have been needed.

Was the Mayan "city," then, an urban complex or a ceremonial center? The conclusions drawn from the excavation of Tikal seem ambiguous. Tikal was surely something more than a religious center, because there is evidence that a rather large population did live there at one time. But it cannot be considered a real urban center either. One can only say that a certain number of individuals — priests, slaves and functionaries perhaps — lived there permanently and depended on outlying areas for their sustenance.

These contradictions and this inexactitude may be disturbing, but it seems relevant to note that a great number of Central American Indians, especially in Guatemala, have lived for thousands of years on small elevated areas in groups of five or six huts. These tiny villages are separated from one another by several acres of land used for the planting and cultivation of maize, and for about every hundred inhabitants there is a meeting place for religious ceremonies.

The Holy Center

After the Spanish Conquest, most of the "privileged" places, or ceremonial centers in Central America, were replaced by a village proper, with a large market square and Christian church, which was usually built on the ruins of the ancient Indian temple. Nevertheless, as few as one hundred people generally live in the villages, while ten thousand inhabitants from nearby lands meet there for religious festivities. On the other hand, these same Indians provide the labor for the upkeep of the church and the village — a type of "voluntary" work, unpaid and obligatory, which is considered an honor.

There are certain obscure points about the large ancient centers of the Mayan culture that archaeology alone cannot explain. One of these is the absence of any type of bastion or defense system in the Petén sites. The classical Mayan site is a holy city, a meeting place for worship and offerings, that is neither a refuge nor a citadel. Hence the vast open spaces in front of the pyramids were fundamental for

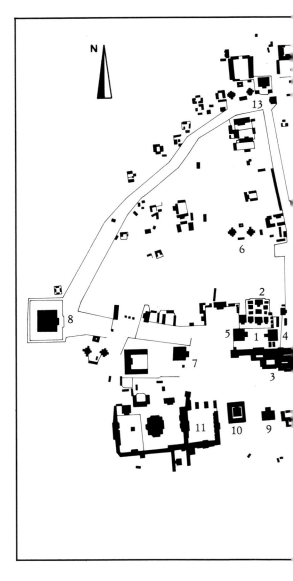

Tikal: General Plan
1. *Great Plaza*
2. *Northern Acropolis*
3. *Central Acropolis*
4. *Temple I*
5. *Temple II*
6. *Architectural complexes of the identical pyramids, O, R, and Q.*
7. *Temple III*
8. *Temple IV*
9. *Temple V*
10. *Southern Acropolis*
11. *Plaza of the Seven Temples*
12. *Group G*
13. *Group H*
14. *Temple of the Inscriptions*

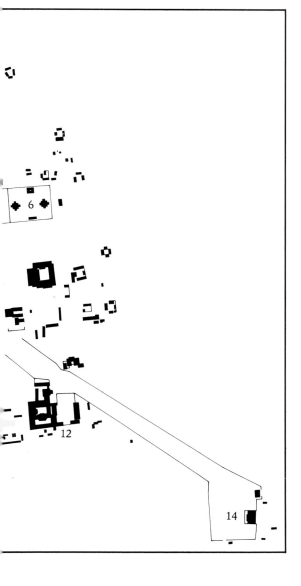

Tikal as well as elsewhere — created for the crowds of worshippers who must have gathered there. The few paved roads that have been found, so strange in a civilization that had neither draft animals nor the wheel, were built for long religious processions.

All around the architectural structures of Tikal lies the dense forest, and it has been difficult for scholars to discover why the ancient Maya settled here. There appears to be no water supply near Tikal, and while the forest in this area is rich in varied species of trees, the land is covered by a mere ten-inch layer of humus and is not favorable for agriculture. According to the archaeological remains, the Maya resolved the problem of water supply by constructing huge wells and reservoirs to collect the abundant rain water.

Thorough archaeological excavations indicate a long settlement of Tikal. It was inhabited from at least 600 B.C. on, a fact that disproves the once commonly held notion that the first Maya cities spontaneously and suddenly appeared in the fourth century A.D., a period fixed by commemorative dates inscribed on various Mayan monuments. The excavation report of the University of Pennsylvania notes that the inhabitants of Tikal must have used local deposits of flint for tools. Including the wood used for construction, which was not very abundant in a place so far from any river, the resources at Tikal were rather meager, and do not appear to account for the development of such a brilliant civilization as that suggested by a site like Tikal. While many specialists agree that the cultivation of maize was a major contribution of this civilization, no discovery has ever confirmed this assertion.

Another hypothesis has been that the Maya did not cut down the trees in order to cultivate maize, but rather to gather the secretion of diverse plants: rubber, chicle, and copal. Petén offers a large supply of such plants, many of which produce excellent incense, which was precious to the Indians because it was destined for the gods. Perfumed resins were apparently indispensable for the complex rites of the theocratic civilizations in other regions of Central America where the essence-producing plants did not grow, and it could be that the essences were exported by the Mayas. Ethnographical observations support this hypothesis, but no conclusion has been agreed upon. Following this line of thought, however, we may imagine that every Mayan city, culturally similar to the others but politically independent, could have become the supplier of a particular incense — given a "brand-name," so to speak, before being exported. The resultant trade would have increased the wealth of those who dealt in it; and those people, free from the need to cultivate, could import maize and could have at their disposal the time and labor necessary for great architectural achievements.

The vision of the past offered by the excavations of Tikal shows the birth, the uncertainties, and the flowering of a civilization during a period of over a thousand years. The very first constructions, small in number, were erected on a small elevated natural area which later became the heart of the city. This confirms an observation made in all the Mayan regions: the villages were built purposely on elevated land, natural or artificial.

Another fundamental point the excavations have taught is that the Maya demolished their monuments at times in order to build new ones on the same site; sometimes they erected a new edifice on top of the old one, without changing the latter. On the Northern Acropolis at Tikal, the ruins consist of a dozen versions placed over ancient constructions, from time to time taken apart and then reconstructed, from the second century A.D. onward. The Great Plaza at Tikal consists of four successive layers, the first dating from 150 B.C., the last from A.D. 700. Most of the structures have been rebuilt many times, but there is no general rule as to when or why. The number of reconstructions and their dates vary for every important monument.

Historians have confirmed that the fifteenth and sixteenth century Aztecs also demolished their temples to build new ones — but at very specific times: at the end of every fifty-two-year cycle. The pyramid of

Tikal: Northern Acropolis. Archaeological excavations reveal a series of overlaid structures, built in the same place over a period of a thousand years. The visible edifices were built in the eighth century A.D., when the architectural complex was modified for the last time.

Tikal: Plan of the Northern Acropolis complex. Numbers 1 to 9 correspond to remains known as structures 20 to 28 respectively. Numbers 10 to 13 correspond to structures 32, 33, 34, and 35.

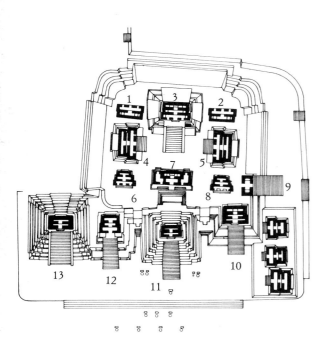

CREATION MYTH OF THE QUICHÉ MAYA

This is the account of how all was in suspense, all calm, in silence; all motionless, still, and the expanse of the sky was empty.

This is the first account, the first narrative. There was neither man, nor animal, birds, fishes, crabs, trees, stones, caves, ravines, grasses, nor forests; there was only the sky.

The surface of the earth had not appeared. There was only the calm sea and the great expanse of the sky.

There was nothing brought together, nothing which could make a noise, nor anything which might move, or tremble, or could make noise in the sky.

There was nothing standing; only the calm water, the placid sea, alone and tranquil. Nothing existed.

There was only immobility and silence in the darkness, in the night. Only the Creator, the Maker, Tepeu, Gucumatz, the Forefathers, were in the water surrounded with light. They were hidden under green and blue feathers, and were therefore called Gucumatz. By nature they were great sages and great thinkers. In this manner the sky existed and also the Heart of Heaven, which is the name of God and thus He is called.

POPOL VUH
(pp. 81–82)

Tenayuca, near Mexico City, with its five constructions built one over the other, is a magnificent subject of study for the historian and the archaeologist. Thousands of miles and more than a millennium separate the first constructions of Mayan and Aztec civilizations, however, and the relationship between them is not known. Another custom verified by excavations at Tikal is that the Maya set out offerings under the base of the stelae, in the foundations of the temples, and inside buildings under construction. Among the offerings that have been found are many obsidian chips (volcanic stone probably imported from the Guatemalan mountains); local flint shaped into a trident, a disc, a half-moon; sea shells; and jade fragments and pearls.

The most disturbing custom of the builders of Tikal is what appears to be the burial of the city's dignitaries in the foundations of demolished buildings ready to be reconstructed. This leads to the supposition that the death of certain dignitaries required a demolition of the edifices that were used during their lifetime. At Tikal there are more than a hundred such tombs, whose furnishings reveal information about various stages of Mayan history.

The history of Tikal began in the sixth century B.C. and continued up to the tenth century A.D., the date of the unexplained disappearance of the Maya from most of the highland sites. There are two phases of these sixteen centuries: the end of the pre-classic period (600 B.C. –A.D. 300) and the classic period (A.D. 300–900). (The post-classic period in Mayan culture refers to sites predominantly in the Yucatán. This latest period ranges from A.D. 900 to the Spanish Conquest.) These divisions are in turn subdivided into shorter periods, each of which may be characterized by a particular style of pottery that has been found on the site:

Eb Pottery. (600 B.C. — 500 B.C.). Attracted by flint deposits and perhaps by the elevation of the land, the first inhabitants settled at Tikal. Deep openings in the limestone bed of the earth reveal not only Eb pots, a human cranium (perhaps decapitated?) and a skeleton in a crouching position, but also fresh water snail shells and pieces of flint, obsidian, and quartz. The flint is of local origin, but the latter two must have been imported. Fragments of charcoal were found that date back to 588 B.C. according to chemical analysis.

Tzac Pottery. (500 B.C. — 300 B.C.). Unfortunately this style has revealed no information about the corresponding historic period.

Chuen Pottery. (300 B.C. — 200 B.C.). During this century the occupation of Tikal seems to have spread over a wider area, and brick architecture with stucco surfacing appeared. The relief-decorated panel, characteristic of all Mayan constructions, flourished, and platform constructions and stucco-decorated temples mirrored the power of king-priests. Evidence indicates that the first demolitions and reconstructions of structures *in situ* took place about this time.

Cauac Pottery. (150 B.C. — A.D. 200). This period was characterized by the appearance of new decorative forms and motifs in pottery. From 50 B.C. on, reliefs representing the jaguar mask decorated the panels of the edifices. Vaulted pyramid and temple structures appeared. This was the period of the first ritual offerings found in the edifices and of the first tomb excavated in the old foundations (Structure 10, Tomb 166).

Cimi Pottery. (A.D. 200–300). This brief phase announced the coming of the classical period. A new form of pottery appeared, perhaps indicating external influences that came from a more evolved civilization. Excavations from this period reveal that the characteristics of the classical period were already in gestation — characteristics such as the massive construction of the temples, polychrome stucco reliefs and figures of jaguars and serpents, corbel-vaulted tombs, stone sculpture, and signs of trade with foreigners. Only writing is missing, although perhaps the writing was done on perishable material.

Muluc Pottery. (A.D. 300–600). Here, in the classical period, a slow evolution of architectural forms took place. The outer walls of the pyramids became covered with magnificent reliefs, their steps flanked by gigantic masks of divinities with the attributes of the jaguar and the serpent. A tiled pediment was added to the temple. This was, above all, the period of hieroglyphic writing. Practically all the classical monuments in Tikal, as in other Mayan cities, were covered with hieroglyphic signs. Stone altars and stelae rose at the foot of the temples.

Tikal is one of the few Mayan sites that shows the evolution of one of the major characteristics of Mayan art: the stone stelae. At first the stelae were narrow blocks with smooth sides. On one of the sides there was a personage, a king-priest or priest-warrior, and on the other was inscribed a hieroglyphic text (Stelae 4, 18, 29). Later, the contours of the figure invaded the sides of the monolith and the text was found on the back (Stelae 1, 2, 28). From A.D. 475 on, smooth-backed stelae appeared, with hieroglyphic inscriptions sculpted on the sides (Stelae 3, 6, 7, 8, 9, 13, 15, 27). Finally, from A.D. 525 on, hieroglyphics covered the stelae except for the principal face (Stelae 14, 23, 25, 31). During the course of the fifth century, motifs from the

THE CREATION OF THE ANIMALS

Then they made the small wild animals, the guardians of the woods, the spirits of the mountains, the deer, the birds, pumas, jaguars, serpents, snakes, vipers, guardians of the thickets.

And the Forefathers asked: "Shall there be only silence and calm under the trees, under the vines? It is well that hereafter there be someone to guard them."

So they said when they meditated and talked. Promptly the deer and the birds were created. Immediately they gave homes to the deer and the birds. "You, deer, shall sleep in the fields by the river bank and in the ravines. Here you shall be amongst the thicket, amongst the pasture; in the woods you shall multiply, you shall walk on four feet and they will support you. Thus be it done!" So it was they spoke.

Then they also assigned homes to the birds big and small. "You shall live in the trees and in the vines. There you shall make your nests; there you shall multiply; there you shall increase in the branches of the trees and in the vines." Thus the deer and the birds were told; they did their duty at once, and all sought their homes and their nests.

And the creation of all the four-footed animals and the birds being finished, they were told by the Creator and the Maker and the Forefathers: "Speak, cry, warble, call, speak each one according to your variety, each, according to your kind." So was it said to the deer, the birds, pumas, jaguars, and serpents.

But they could not make them speak like men; they only hissed and screamed and cackled; they were unable to make words, and each screamed in a different way.

When the Creator and the Maker saw that it was impossible for them to talk to each other, they said: "It is impossible for them to say our names, the names of us, their Creators and Makers. This is not well," said the Forefathers to each other.

Then they said to them: "Because it has not been possible for you to talk, you shall be changed. We have changed our minds: Your food, your pasture, your homes, and your nests you shall have; they shall be the ravines and the woods, because it has not been possible for you to adore us or invoke us. There shall be those who adore us, we shall make other beings who shall be obedient. Accept your destiny: your flesh shall be torn to pieces. So shall it be. This shall be your lot." So they said, when they made known their will to the large and small animals which are on the face of the earth.

They wished to give them another trial; they wished to make another attempt; they wished to make all living things adore them.

But they could not understand each other's speech; they could succeed in nothing, and could do nothing. For this reason they were sacrificed, and the animals which were on earth were condemned to be killed and eaten.

For this reason another attempt had to be made to create and make man by the Creator, the Maker, and the Forefathers.

POPOL VUH
(pp. 84–86)

Tikal: Stele 9. It is dated 9.2.0.0.0. (A.D. 475). The style and disposition of the bas-reliefs suggest that this stele belonged to a group of monuments built between 475 and 500. One simply dressed person decorates the principal face; hieroglyphs appear on the two sides, and the back portion is smooth.

Tikal: Stele 10. This is the only stele in the city that has never fallen. It is very corroded. Any deciphering of the glyphs is difficult and uncertain, but they seem to indicate the date 09.3.13.0.0. (A.D. 507).

central Mexican civilization of Teotihuacán became evident. This city had established a colony on the plateaus of Guatemala in the fourth century, and began to exert some influence on Mayan architecture during the next few centuries. Perhaps the borrowed motifs demonstrate that the leaders of Tikal wanted to leave traces of the relationship they established with this great city of central Mexico, more than twelve hundred miles away.

Ik Pottery. (A.D. 600–650). This first phase of the late classical period manifested considerable changes in pottery, which from this time on was splendidly painted and covered with hieroglyphic bands. At the same time, classical Mayan architecture appeared to lose its exuberance and became more sober.

Imix Pottery. (A.D. 650–900). The last phase of the late classical period was dominated by a profusion of edifices and a splendor of the arts, after which there was at Tikal an inexplicable disappearance of most evidence of Mayan culture. In the tenth century there was, apparently, a sudden abandonment of all the great cities of Petén. The latest stele to be found (Number 11) was erected in 879.

The Pyramids

The pyramids of Tikal, which can still be admired, were built in a rather late classical period, in the eighth century. These are the largest monuments in Mayan territory. Archaeological evidence indicates that these structures dominated Tikal for an entire century, and then witnessed its desertion and the invasion of the forest without undergoing either destruction or reconstruction. Also, unlike many previous edifices, the pyramids were not built on the ruins of other constructions.

An ornamental breastplate of jade that dates from about A.D. 750; it was found at Nebaj, Guatemala. (Guatemala City, La Aurora Museum.)

THE CREATION OF MAN AND WOMAN

Then was the creation and the formation. Of earth, of mud, they made man's flesh. But they saw that it was not good. It melted away, it was soft, did not move, had no strength, it fell down, it was limp, it could not move its head, its face fell to one side, its sight was blurred, it could not look behind. At first it spoke, but had no mind. Quickly it soaked in the water and could not stand.

And the Creator and the Maker said: "Let us try again because our creatures will not be able to walk nor multiply. Let us consider this," they said.

Then they broke up and destroyed their work and their creation. And they said: "What shall we do to perfect it, in order that our worshipers, our invokers, will be successful?" . . . .

And instantly the figures were made of wood. They looked like men, talked like men, and populated the surface of the earth.

They existed and multiplied; they had daughters, they had sons, these wooden figures; but they did not have souls, nor minds, they did not remember their Creator, their Maker; they walked on all fours, aimlessly.

They no longer remembered the Heart of Heaven and therefore they fell out of favor. It was merely a trial, an attempt at man. At first they spoke, but their face was without expression; their feet and hands had no strength; they had no blood, nor substance, nor moisture, nor flesh; their cheeks were dry, their feet and hands were dry, and their flesh was yellow.

Therefore, they no longer thought of their Creator nor their Maker, nor of those who made them and cared for them.

These were the first men who existed in great numbers on the face of the earth. . . .

Immediately the wooden figures were annihilated, destroyed, broken up, and killed.

A flood was brought about by the Heart of Heaven; a great flood was formed which fell on the heads of the wooden creatures. Of *tzité*, the flesh of man was made, but when woman was fashioned by the Creator and the Maker, her flesh was made of rushes. These were the materials the Creator and the Maker wanted to use in making them.

But those that they had made, that they had created, did not think, did not speak with their Creator, their Maker. And for this reason they were killed, they were deluged. A heavy resin fell from the sky. The one called Xecotcovach came and gouged out their eyes; Camalotz came and cut off their heads; Cotzbalam came and devoured their flesh. Tucumbalam came, too, and broke and mangled their bones and their nerves, and ground and crumbled their bones.

This was to punish them because they had not thought of their mother, nor their father, the Heart of Heaven, called Huracán. And for this reason the face of the earth was darkened and a black rain began to fall, by day and by night.

POPOL VUH
(pp. 86-87)

The Mayan pyramid was not a tomb, and nothing relates it to the Egyptian structure which served as a sepulcher for the pharaoh — a forbidden dominion which no one could enter after the dead king and his retinue were buried there. The ziggurat, temple of the ancient Sumerians, built in step-pyramid form with a sanctuary-observatory on the top, is actually the monument that most resembles a Mayan pyramid. It is useless to make comparisons between the Mayan and Sumerian civilizations, however. Besides the great distance, these two types of pyramid are separated by four thousand years and the materials used for their construction are different. The Sumerians did not have stone, and so fired millions of mud bricks, later stuck together with bitumen, to construct the gigantic bases for their temples. On the other hand, the Maya were fortunate enough to live in an area that supplied not only building stone, but also the limestone used in cement.

Perhaps more than any other technical innovation, it was the discovery and use of cement that allowed the Maya to express themselves with such bold architecture. In Uaxactún, a secondary site that must have been a satellite of Tikal, traces of the "birth" of the pyramids were found by archaeologists more than thirty years ago. Originally, the pyramids were simply a modest mound of bricks used to support a temple, which was at that time a simple hut. (The need to elevate a sanctuary is common to all religions — as in Christian communities, where village and country churches dominate the houses.) Over the years, a brick base was added to the primitive embankment, and this base was gradually raised higher, making it necessary to build stairs to reach the temple. The pyramid form then grew progressively with the raised temple.

Since the function of Mayan pyramids was to support the temple, they were always flat-topped. The heart of the pyramid consisted of an amalgamation of stones and clay tightly compressed by a brick casing. The more daring the pyramid became, the more complex its technical problems. The great challenge to the Mayans must have been the construction of the nearly vertical pyramid at Tikal, 130 feet high with a 100-foot base. In order to erect the enormous bases of Temples I, II, III and IV at Tikal, the builders abandoned a stone and clay nucleus. Rather, they built platforms on top of each other. The interiors of these gigantic pyramids contained square or rectangular blocks of stone, carefully and accurately set up to fit in the supporting walls. The surface of the platform was then cemented over, and a casing, or layer, of thin brickwork covering the entire pyramid served more as decoration than as protection.

Rudimentary steps, which must have been built little by little as the pyramid increased in height, were demolished as soon as the construction was completed, and a final staircase without ramps was built. Workmen building the temple on the last terrace must have used this staircase, and the Mayans believed that the priests used it in order to approach the gods (just as the gods, supposedly, used it to descend to the crowds who gathered for the religious festivals.) At the top of the pyramid, the temple was decorated with a tiled and perforated gable or "roof comb," and contained two or three dark narrow chambers each with an area of only about sixty square feet. The magnificence of the supporting pyramid quite outdid the edifice for which it was built. A link "between the earth and the sky," the pyramid became for the Mayans something more than an answer to a technical challenge: it was a religious necessity. The pyramid was without a doubt a precious aid for the highly-respected priest-astronomer of the Mayan culture, who must have been eager to perfect his knowledge of the movement of the stars in order to predict the future.

Copán

Copán lies at the southeastern end of the Mayan territory, in Honduras. Its geographic position is more than 250 miles from Tikal, and its geological and climatic conditions, so different from those in Petén, make it a unique site. The land around Copán is more fertile, though still mountainous, and the climate is milder; human settlement and civilization might be more expected in such an area. Some scholars have even asserted that Copán was the starting point of the Mayan civilization, since its natural conditions are so favorable. Here, they say, the Mayan culture first took root and then spread into Petén. Doubt has been cast on this theory by several findings, however, including the fact that the hieroglyphic inscriptions on the monuments in Tikal bear the earliest date: A.D. 292. In Copán, the earliest recorded date is A.D. 460.

Copán is interesting because of its sculpture, especially its handsome stelae, and also because of its splendid staircases and a profusion of hieroglyphics. This site is thought to have been the scientific center of the classical Mayan period, possibly specializing in astronomy. According to certain authorities, the establishment of this site was due not to the richness of the soil but to its clear, limpid skies. A relatively high altitude (about 2,000 feet) and a wide, open valley permitted regular and precise astronomical observations. The Maya had no optical instruments for such observations, but they did use jade tubes (to assist them in concentrating their vision) and they calculated the revolutions of Venus and predicted eclipses with amazing precision. The many hieroglyphs concerning these phenomena are particularly important in Copán and confirm its role as a scientific center.

Panorama of the Site

Situated in this large valley in Honduras, 1,500 miles long and eight miles wide, Copán's main group of structures takes up about sixty acres. There are five principal open spaces, or plazas.

To the north lies the acropolis, with its two plazas oriented north to south. A platform forty feet high dominates the center of the acropolis, which covers five acres of land. The eastern square, 130 feet by 100 feet, is flanked on the west by a large pyramid (Number 16) and the Jaguar Stairway — which owes its name to two large stone jaguars set on the sides of eight steps that extend fifty-two feet across. (Fragments of obsidian on the two sculptures give a spotted effect to the coat of the animal.) Evidence of a jaguar cult in the Mayan civilization has been found in sculpture on pre-classical edifices at Tikal, and the jaguar is represented again and again at Copán. Bas-reliefs at the site of Yaxchilán also appear to confirm the existence of a "Priest of Jaguar." The top of the stairway is dominated by the colossal head of a person representing the sun, adorned with the symbol of Venus. On the eastern side of the eastern square there are three ruined temples: Numbers 18, 19, and 20. The remains of Temples 21 and 22 lie to the south. The entrance to Temple 22, consecrated in A.D. 771 to the planet Venus, is

ANCESTORS OF THE
QUICHÉ MAYA

These are the names of the first men who were created and formed: the first man was Balam-Quitzé, the second, Balam-Acab, the third, Mahucutah, and the fourth was Iqui-Balam.

These are the names of our first mothers and fathers.

It is said that they only were made and formed, they had no mother, they had no father. They were only called men. They were not born of woman, nor were they begotten by the Creator nor by the Maker, nor by the Forefathers. Only by a miracle, by means of incantation were they created and made by the Creator, the Maker, the Forefathers, Tepeu and Gucumatz. And as they had the appearance of men, they were men, they talked, conversed, saw and heard, walked, grasped things; they were good and handsome men, and their figure was the figure of a man.

They were endowed with intelligence; they saw and instantly they could see far, they succeeded in seeing, they succeeded in knowing all that there is in the world. When they looked, instantly they saw all around them, and they contemplated in turn the arch of heaven and the round face of the earth.

The things hidden in the distance they saw all, without first having to move; at once they saw the world, and so, too, from where they were, they saw it.

Great was their wisdom; their sight reached to the forests, the rocks, the lakes, the seas, the mountains, and the valleys. In truth, they were admirable men, Balam-Quitzé, Balam-Acab, Mahucutah, and Iqui-Balam.

POPOL VUH
(pp. 167–68)

Copán: Colossal stone head, situated on a step of the stairway in the eastern plaza of the acropolis. It probably represents the great god Itzamná, the inventor of writing and calendars.

Copán: General plan.
1. Acropolis
2. Tumulus 4
3. Plaza of the Hieroglyphic Stairway
4. Western Plaza
5. Eastern Plaza
6. Pyramid 16
7. Jaguar Stairway
8. Terrace 17
9, 10, 11, 12. Temples 18, 19, 20, 21.
13. Temple 22
14. Temple 13
15. Temple 14
16. Spectators' Grandstand
17. Temple 11
18. Temple 26 (with the Hieroglyphic Stairway)
19. Ball court
20. Stele H
21. Stele B
22. Altar Q
23. Río (River) Copán

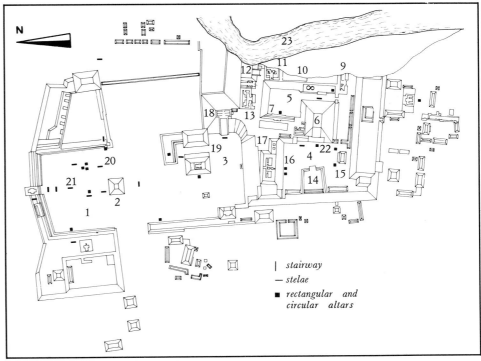

| stairway
— stelae
■ rectangular and circular altars

decorated on both sides with a high-relief sculpture made of connecting tiles, which represents animals, human figures, and serpents. The tile panel rests, on both sides of the entrance, upon large realistic skulls that possibly represent the Mayan god of death, *Ah Puch*.

The western square in Copán is 230 feet long and 75 feet wide. Temple 13, to the west, and Temple 14, to the south, are a short distance from each other. To the east, friezes of human skulls decorate the first four steps of a stairway that goes up to the top of Pyramid 16. To the north of the square, the second section of a stairway that leads to the ruins of Temple 11 is known as the Spectators' Grandstand. The sixth and final step of this stairway is completely covered with hiero- glyphs and is guarded on both sides by two powerful-looking kneeling figures with leonine heads. A serpent wriggles from their lips, and in their left hand they brandish a torch bearing the symbol of the rain god; in their right hand they hold a mass of writhing serpents. The meaning of these sculptures is not known. (According to Sylvanus G. Morley, a prominent Maya scholar, Temple 11 was erected in 764 to

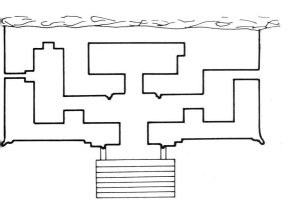

Copán: Plan of Temple 22. Stone bas-reliefs depicting fantastic animals decorate the communicating door between the first and second rooms.

commemorate an important discovery made at Copán: the exact duration of the intervals between the lunar eclipses.)

At the two northern corners of Temple 11, archaeologists have found two gigantic human heads of stone. Various sculpture pieces of this type have been found on the acropolis, and they have been given the name "old man of Copán." They could be different incarnations of one of the greatest Mayan gods, Itzamná — sometimes represented as a toothless old man, bearded, with sunken features and an aquiline nose. According to Bishop de Landa's sixteenth century report, this god was the ruler of the Mayan pantheon, was the first high priest, and was the inventor of Mayan writing.

South of the acropolis, a stairway rising at a sixty-degree angle to a height of eighty-six feet, leads to the ruins of Temple 26. The sixty-three steps to this temple, which measure thirty feet across, are completely sculpted in hieroglyphic inscriptions. Low ramps, three feet wide and decorated with birds and serpents, rise on both sides of the steps, and statues of noble-looking men appear in the center of the stairway at

Left:
Copán: Panorama of the Sacred Ball Court north of the plaza of the Hieroglyphic Stairway. The first foundations bear the date A.D. 514. Two sharply inclined cemented bases border the courtyard (85 × 23 feet).

Right:
Copán: Hieroglyphic Stairway. The 2,500 signs sculpted on the steps represent the longest hieroglyphic inscription found in Mayan territory. The steps bear twenty-eight dates, from A.D. 545 to 745.

Below:
Copán: Stele 5, situated at the entrance to the archaeological zone.

This annulus in the center of the disk is white and indicates the course of the sun. Between the two rings the black spots indicate the face of the sun, which goes over the large black one and descends to the small black one. Thus its movement is uniform, and this is its course here on earth also. On the ground it is thus manifested plainly all over the earth also. The progress of the sun is truly great as it takes its course to enter into the great *Oro* extended over the world. This is the record of the motion of the sun as it is known here on earth.

To the people on the sides of this half-section as pictured, the sun is not eclipsed; but for anyone who is in the middle it is eclipsed. It is in conjunction with the moon when it is eclipsed. It travels in its course before it is eclipsed. It arrives in its course to the north, very great. It is all the same with eclipses of the sun and moon before it arrives opposite to the sun. This is the explanation so that Maya people may know what happens to the sun and to the moon.

The Book of the Chilam Balam of Chumayel
(p. 87)

THE INTERROGATION OF THE CHIEFS

This is the examination which takes place in the katun which ends today. The time has arrived for examining the knowledge of the chiefs of the towns, to see whether they know how the ruling men came, whether they have explained the coming of the chiefs, of the head-chiefs, whether they are of the lineage of rulers, whether they are of the lineage of chiefs, that they may prove it.

This is the first question which will be asked of them: he shall ask them for his food "Bring the sun." This is the word of the head-chief to them; thus it is said to the chiefs. "Bring the sun, my son, bear it on the palm of your hand to my plate. A lance is planted, a lofty cross, in the middle of its heart. A green jaguar is seated over the sun to drink its blood." Of Zuyua is the wisdom. This is what the sun is which is demanded of them: a very large fried egg. This is the lance and the lofty cross planted in its heart of which he speaks: it is the benediction. This is what the green jaguar is which is set over it to drink its blood: it is a green chile-pepper, is the jaguar. This is the language of Zuyua.

The Book of Chilam Balam of Chumayel
(pp. 89–90)

Copán: Stele C, cut from andesite like all the stelae in this city. It bears the date 9.17.12.0.0., or A.D. 782. Another personage with a beard appears on the back side of this stele. The personages represented on the Copán stelae are apparently high dignitaries, not gods.

intervals of every twelve steps. This stairway, known as the Hieroglyphic Stairway, contains 2,500 signs and represents the largest single collection of inscriptions in the Mayan world. The dates recorded in the hieroglyphs range from A.D. 545 to 745.

A ball court, which is one of the main structures in most classical Mayan centers, lies north of the plaza from which the Hieroglyphic Stairway rises. The court, which dates from about A.D. 300, is eighty-eight feet long and twenty-three feet wide, flanked all along its length by sharply inclining cement bases. Three stylized parrot heads, at equal distance from one another, keep watch over the ball court area. This complex is elongated by two vast adjacent areas flanked on three sides by long tiers of stone seats — the grandstand for the crowd that must have congregated in Copán for great religious festivities. (A description of the ball game will be given in a later chapter.)

On the following pages:
Copán: Altar G, depicting two two-headed serpents. In the center, Stele H, erected in A.D. 782. The dignitary sculptured on this monument is wearing a tunic, the only example of its kind in Copán.

Copán: A stone altar depicting the god of death, Ah Puch.

The Stelae

A marvelous series of carved stelae, or monoliths, adorn the plaza mentioned above. The stelae are the glory of Copán, and scholars have wondered if some unusual position of the site favored the development of such a high quality of art.

Copán contains thirty-eight stelae, fourteen of which stand on the central plaza. The latter are the most remarkable. As high as thirteen feet and five feet wide, made of andesitic rock, these stelae bear majestic figures on their principal side, sculpted in high relief. All known types of Mayan stelae can be found at Copán — with one, two, three, or all four sides sculpted. Generally, the Copán stelae have a personage on each of the two main sides.

A close examination of the stelae reveals great technical prowess. The Copán sculptors knew how to represent their figures entirely with the face; the anatomic proportions of the faces are accurate, while the shapes of the bodies disappear under vestments. Large headdresses cover the heads, and little surface space is void of decoration. The stelae depicting seated figures reveal exceptional skill in portraiture.

Certain peculiarities of the Copán stelae have been described in great detail, and many theories about them have been advanced. One such theory is that Stele H depicts a female figure, because the personage depicted wears a skirt, while figures on other stelae wear girdles. In reality, this skirt is probably a simple tunic — thought to be the typical and traditional dress of priests of certain cults. Stele B is another source of various interpretations. Two stylized macaws decorate the upper part of this monolith, and some observers claim to recognize the trunk of an elephant in the birds' beaks.

Most of the figures on the Copán stelae appear to be very young. Others have a beard — an interesting fact for a supposedly beardless people. Sources of information gathered in the Yucatán after the Spanish Conquest say that the Mayans there considered beards unseemly; they would burn the cheeks and chins of their young with boiling water to eliminate any growth of hairs. It could be that in Copán in the classical period, a beard was a symbol of power or authority and was reserved for a small number of persons. Or, it could be that this representation was actually a false beard — such as those worn by the pharaohs of Egypt. The subject is still open to discussion.

At Copán, as in all the Mayan sites, it is believed that the stelae were constructed to appease the gods, to represent the civil and religious dignitaries of the time, and to mark the passage of time. The figures on the stelae are imposing, unlike each other except for a ceremonial stick, held in their crossed arms, which represents a highly stylized two-headed serpent that has been difficult to identify. In Central America the serpent image is closely connected with the cult of time and calculations; often it represents the vault of heaven. Thus the ceremonial stick in Copán might have been the emblem of the culture's priest-astronomers. At the foot of the stelae, sculpted stone blocks — sometimes in bizarre forms — received offerings and sacrifices. The most unusual one, Altar Q, bears the construction date of 775 (the first inscription discovered and annotated by Stephens in Copán). This "altar" is a square block, four-and-a-half feet long and twenty-seven inches high; on each side, four figures sit cross-legged on top of a hieroglyph, holding an object similar to a book in their right hand. According to some experts, the bas-relief depicts a meeting of priest-astronomers.

What is the exact meaning of these stelae? As in other Mayan centers, the stelae seem like enigmatic sphinxes whose function must surely have been more than commemorative. They are covered with lavish hieroglyphics, many of which are still indecipherable. It could be that the signs on each monolith represent an esoteric text reserved for certain initiates. If so, these annotations could contain the key to the cultural enigmas of the Mayan civilization. In any case, they serve as a link between all the holy sites of the Maya, and are undeniable proof of the high level of civilization reached by these people.

THE FIRST STORIES OF THE CAKCHIQUELS

Here I shall write a few stories of our first fathers and ancestors, those who begot man of old, before these mountains and valleys were inhabited, when there were only rabbits and birds, so they said; when our fathers and grandfathers went to populate the mountains and valleys, oh, my sons! in Tulán.

I shall write the stories of our first fathers and grandfathers, one of whom was called Gagavitz, the other Zactecauh; the stories that they told to us; that from the other side of the sea we came to the place called Tulán, where we were begotten and given birth by our mothers and our fathers, oh, our sons!

Thus they related of yore, the fathers and grandfathers who were called Gagavitz and Zactecauh, those who came to Tulán, the two men who begot us, the Xahilá.

The Annals of the Cakchiquels
(p. 72)

THE MIGRATION NARRATIVE

These are the names of whatever towns there were and the names of the wells, in order that it may be known where they passed in their march to see whether this district was good, whether it was suitable for settlement here. They set in order the names of the district according to the command of our Lord God. He it was who set the land in order. He created everything on earth. He set it in order also. But these were the people who named the district, who named the wells, who named the villages, who named the land because no one had arrived here in this neck of the land when we arrived here.

Zubinche, Kaua, Cumcanul (Cuncunul), Tiemtun (Ebtun) ,where the precious stones descended, Zizal, Zacii (Valladolid), Ticooc (Tesoco), where the law of the katun was fulfilled, Timozon, Popola, where the mat of the katun was spread, Tipixoy (Pixoy), Uayumhaa (Uayma), Zacbacelcan, Tinum where little was said to them, Timacal, Popola where they counted the mat of the katun in its order . . . .

The Book of Chilam Balam of Chumayel
(p. 43)

THE THREATS OF THE TRIBES

Now, then, many towns were being founded, one by one, and the different branches of the tribes were being reunited and settled close to the roads, their roads which they had opened.

As for Balam-Quitzé, Balam-Acab, Mahucutah, and Iqui-Balam, it was not known where they were. But when they saw the tribes that passed on the roads, instantly they began to shout on the mountain-tops, howling like a coyote, screaming like a mountain cat, and imitating the roaring of the puma and the jaguar.

And the tribes seeing these things, as they walked, said: "Their screams are like those of the coyote, of the mountain cat, of the puma, and of the jaguar. They want to appear to the tribes as though they are not men, and they only do this to deceive us, we the people. Their hearts wish something. Surely, they do not frighten us with what they do. They mean something with the roaring of the puma, with the noise of the jaguar which they break into when they see one or two men walking; what they want is to make an end of us."

POPOL VUH
(p. 193)

The Hieroglyphs

In 1841, when John L. Stephens explored Copán, he hoped that the hieroglyphics on the stelae would give precise indications about the civilization he had discovered. When Brasseur de Bourbourg, about twenty years later, found Bishop de Landa's sixteenth century record of the Mayas at the Madrid Royal Library, everyone believed that the "Rosetta Stone" of Mayan writing had been discovered. Thirty-five pages of Landa's work contain drawings of hieroglyphic signs, accompanied by their meaning in Spanish. Since these signs are similar to a great number of those inscribed on stones of the classical Maya monuments, experts began to believe that they had undeniable proof of the cultural relationship between the Indians of the Yucatán and the ancient builders of the classical Maya sites in Petén. Unfortunately, the signs in Landa's book merely represent months, years, days, time cycles, and numbers, with explanations of the part they played in Mayan calendar systems. As for the other writing, Landa dedicated only one page to this. This sixteenth century priest simply could not conceive of a writing that was not alphabetic; he wrote in his text that he had asked the Indians about the phonetic equivalents of certain signs — a mistake that misled research workers for over a century, by limiting them to possible phonetic solutions — whereas Mayan writing might very well be of a completely different nature.

Copán: Temple 11, or Temple of the Inscriptions, built in A.D. 764 to commemorate the discovery of the exact duration of the intervals between the lunar eclipses.

Here, then, is the dawn, and the coming of the sun, the moon, and the stars.

Balam-Quitzé, Balam-Acab, Mahucutah, and Iqui-Balam were very happy when they saw the Morning Star. It rose first, with shining face, when it came ahead of the sun.

Immediately they unwrapped the incense which they had brought from the East, and which they had planned to burn, and then they untied the three gifts which they had planned to offer. . . .

They wept for joy as they danced and burned their incense, their precious incense. Then they wept because they did not yet behold nor see the sunrise.

But, then, the sun came up. The small and large animals were happy; and arose from the banks of the river, in the ravines, and on the tops of the mountains, and all turned their eyes to where the sun was rising.

Then the puma and the jaguar roared. But first the bird called Queletzú burst into song. In truth, all the animals were happy, and the eagle, the white vulture; the small birds and the large birds stretched their wings.

The priests and the sacrificers were kneeling; great was the joy of the priests and sacrificers and of the people of Tamub and Ilocab and the people of Rabinal, the Cakchiquel, those from Tziquinahá, and those from Tuhalhá, Uchabahá, Quibahá, from Batená, and the Yaqui Tepeu, all those tribes which exist today. And it was not possible to count the people. The light of dawn fell upon all the tribes at the same time.

Instantly the surface of the earth was dried by the sun. Like a man was the sun when it showed itself, and its face glowed when it dried the surface of the earth.

Before the sun rose, damp and muddy was the surface of the earth, before the sun came up; but then the sun rose, and came up like a man. And its heat was unbearable. It showed itself when it was born and remained fixed in the sky like a mirror. Certainly it was not the same sun which we see, it is said in their old tales.

Immediately afterward Tohil, Avilix, and Hacavitz were turned to stone, together with the deified beings, the puma, the jaguar, the snake, the cantil, and the hobgoblin. Their arms became fastened to the trees when the sun, the moon, and the stars appeared. All alike, were changed into stone. Perhaps we should not be living today because of the voracious animals, the puma, the jaguar, the snake, and the cantil, as well as the hobgoblin; perhaps our power would not exist if these first animals had not been turned into stone by the sun.

POPOL VUH
(pp. 186–188)

Copán: Stele M, dated 9.16.5.0.0. (A.D. 756). Here, as in the case of all Mayan inscriptions, only the calendar glyphs can be translated, leaving about one-third of the total number indecipherable at present.

PETITIONS TO THE GOD

Here are their petitions to their god, when they prayed; and this was the supplication of their hearts:

"Oh, Thou, beauty of the day! Thou, Huracán; Thou, Heart of Heaven and of Earth! Thou, giver of richness, and giver of the daughters and the sons! Turn toward us your power and your riches; grant life and growth unto my sons and vassals; let those who must maintain and nourish Thee multiply and increase; those who invoke Thee on the roads, in the fields, on the banks of the rivers, in the ravines, under the trees, under the vines.

"Give them daughters and sons. Let them not meet disgrace, nor misfortune, let not the deceiver come behind or before them. Let them not fall, let them not be wounded, let them not fornicate, nor be condemned by justice. Let them not fall on the descent or on the ascent of the road. Let them not encounter obstacles back of them or before them, nor anything which strikes them. Grant them good roads, beautiful, level roads. Let them not have misfortune, nor disgrace, through Thy fault, through Thy sorceries.

"Grant a good life to those who must give Thee sustenance and place food in Thy mouth, in Thy presence, to Thee, Heart of Heaven, Heart of Earth, Bundle of Majesty. And Thou, Tohil; Thou, Avilix; Thou, Hacavitz, Arch of the Sky, Surface of the Earth, the Four Corners, the Four Cardinal Points. Let there be but peace and tranquility in Thy mouth, in Thy presence, oh, God!"

POPOL VUH
(pp. 226–27)

Copán: Stele N, dated 9.16.9.0.0. (A.D. 760). The personage sculptured here has all the attributes typical of a highly religious dignitary. The headdress is large; the girdle, finely decorated, reaches the ground. The dignitary wears jaguar-skin sandals and holds in his hands a ceremonial stick in the form of a two-headed serpent.

In addition to Landa's information on the hieroglyphs, there are three ancient codices covered with Mayan hieroglyphs (dating from the post-classic period) now in the archives of three European libraries (to be described in detail later). Only the calendar notations in these codices have been transcribed, however, and the rest remain undeciphered. Besides hieroglyphs, the codices contain drawings of the gods and scenes of worship and divination. The gods are partially recognizable, thanks to the scenes they are set in and to Landa's book, which lists a great number of gods and gives details regarding their calendar attributes. These attributes are sculpted in the stone of the ancient centers and some identification of the personages they are connected with is possible — at least the name they bore in Yucatán during the Spanish Conquest. Needless to say, the interpretations of these codices and notations are most hypothetical.

All the known Mayan hieroglyphs have been catalogued, but despite this, experts do not agree on their number. In reality, some of the symbols are enlarged with affixes which, in some inscriptions, become

THE POWER OF THE KATUN

Give yourselves up, my younger brothers, my older brothers, submit to the unhappy destiny of the katun which is to come. If you do not submit, you shall be moved from where your feet are rooted. If you do not submit, you shall gnaw the trunks of trees and herbs. If you do not submit, it shall be as when the deer die, so that they go forth from your settlement. Then even when the ruler himself goes forth, he shall return within your settlement bearing nothing. Also there shall come such a pestilence that the vultures enter the houses, a time of great death among the wild animals.

The Book of Chilam Balam of Chumayel
(p. 122)

Katun 8 Ahau came. 8 Ahau was the name of the katun when their government occurred. Then there was a change of the katun, then there was a change of rulers. . . . when our rulers increased in numbers, according to the words of their priest to them. Then they introduced the drought. That which came was a drought, according to their words, when the hoofs of the animals burned, when the seashore burned, a sea of misery. So it was said on high, so it was said. Then the face of the sun was eaten; then the face of the sun was darkened; then its face was extinguished. They were terrified on high, when it burned at the word of their priest to them, when the word of our ruler was fulfilled at the word of their priest to them. Then began the idea of painting the exterior of the sun. When they heard of that, they saw the moon. Then came the rulers of the land. It was Ix-Tziu-nene who introduced sin to us, the slaves of the land, when he came. Then the law of the katun, the divination of the katun shall be fulfilled. When he was brought, what was your command, you, the rulers of the land? Then the law of another katun was introduced, at the end of the katun when Ix-Tziu-nene was brought. Whereupon a numerous army was seen, and they began to be killed. Then a thing of terror was constructed, a gallows for their death. Now began the archery of Ox-halal Chan. Then the rulers of the land were called. Their blood flowed, and it was taken by the archers. They were terrified. . . the time when the katun ended for them. . . .

The Book of Chilam Balam of Chumayel
(pp. 76–77)

THE CHARGE OF KATUN 13 AHAU

The Katun is established at Kinchil Coba, Maya Cuzamil, in Katun 13 Ahau. Itzamná, Itzam-tzab, is his face during its reign. The ramon shall be eaten. Three years shall be locust years, ten generations of locusts. The fan shall be displayed; the bouquet shall be displayed, borne by Yaxaal Chac in the heavens. Unattainable is the bread of the katun in 13 Ahau. The sun shall be eclipsed. Double is the charge of the katun: men without offspring, chiefs without successors. For five days the sun shall be eclipsed, then it shall be seen again. This is the charge of Katun 13 Ahau.

The Book of Chilam Balam of Chumayel
(p. 134)

hieroglyphs proper; on the other hand, there are commonly used "glyphs" which sometimes become affixes. There are approximately eight hundred glyphs, four hundred of which are generally considered fundamental. Such a number is excessive for any phonetic writing. (The English language alphabetic writing has only twenty-six signs, and only about twice this number would be needed for syllabic writing.) On the other hand, there are hardly enough hieroglyphs to represent ideograms or logograms — Chinese writing contains thousands of these. So what can be said? Is Mayan writing only partially phonetic, or is it essentially symbolic, or does it perhaps follow homophonic principles?

In recent years, some Russian students of Mayan writing programmed a computer to try to solve the problem of these hieroglyphs, but so far they have not announced any solution. Moreover, this writing form will probably never be transcribed as long as it is considered the basis of spoken Mayan of the sixteenth century. In reality, the hieroglyphs must be a script that was invented to represent an esoteric or liturgical language reserved for a chosen few. Most experts agree that the Mayan inscriptions have no social or historical context; they are not panegyrics of royal or religious personages, nor are they accounts of war and conquests. Their basic function seems to have been that of registering the date of construction or consecration of the monuments they are inscribed upon.

Because of Landa's book and subsequent scholarly works, about half of the fundamental glyphs can be identified — all of which are related to the recording and measurement of time. The dates in these glyphs are transcribed precisely, and also establish that the Maya had a tradition of building a stele at the end of every *katun*, that is, every twenty-year period. At times, according to the wealth of the area, the construction of a stele took place every half *katun* (*lahuntun*) or even every quarter *katun* (*hotun*). Moreover, from certain explanations of Landa's and other post-Conquest chroniclers, it appears that an imperative rule "obliged" the ancient Maya to erect a stele every twenty years. These monuments thus have become true milestones of time. The ritual necessity to build stelae on precise dates marked the activities of at least a portion of the population and this obligation seems to have remained practically unaltered for the entire duration of the classical period.

In order to calculate and record the passage of time, then, the Maya must have invented mathematics and writing. For centuries they made rigorous astronomical observations and elaborated calendars more precise than the calendars of today. Every period of time — day, month, year, or cycle — was apparently represented by a god set on the shoulders of another god who transported him from one end of the horizon to the other. Time moved tirelessly in the oriented space of the Maya universe. On the stelae, these divinities were sometimes accompanied by the nine gods of night, the *Bolonkitu*, and by the gods of the lunar months and of the Venus and eclipse years. It seems that no people in the world were ever so preoccupied with time.

Quirigúa

Quiriguá, a secondary Mayan site of the humid Motagua River valley, lies east of the road that leads from Guatemala City to Puerto Barrios, thirty miles northeast of Copán. The waters of the Motagua inundate the lands of Quiriguá often, making this valley one of the most fertile in Central America. With heavy rains and torrid heat, Quiriguá is in the midst of a tropical zone.

Few vestiges remain of this city's architecture. Here stelae constitute the essential archaeological evidence, and because the Mayan builders of Quiriguá erected these monoliths at the end of every *hotun* (a five year period), the site offers perhaps the loveliest sequential series of sculpted and dated Mayan stelae. And while Mayan art may appear to be rather static, these stelae reveal gradually evolving differences.

The first of these evolutions relates to size: over the years the stelae became higher and higher. Stele T, one of the first, dates from A.D. 692 and is six feet high. Stele J, dated 756, reaches a height of sixteen feet, and Stele F, dated 761, rises to over twenty-three feet. Finally Stele E, built in 771, is almost thirty-five feet high, weighs over 65 tons and marks the end of a *katun*, or twenty years.

Given the limited technical means of the Maya, who apparently cut stone with diorite blades and wooden mallets, the size of these stelae is a considerable achievement, even if one takes into account the fact that the stone must have been taken from hills only three miles away. After the erection of Stele E, the highest (so far discovered) in Mayan civilization, another evolution seems to take place. Twin Stelae A and C rise to heights of only thirteen and fourteen-and-a-half feet respectively. Both bear the representation of a personage on their front and back sides, but for the first time in Quiriguá, the faces on the back of the stelae face east. They are sculpted in profile and the figures have jaguar paws. The erection of these twin stelae bear the same date — 775.

Other signs of stylistic evolution reveal themselves in the types of insignia for the sculpted figures on the stelae. In Quiriguá, there are the two-headed stick that was in evidence at Copán (which was probably the emblem of the priest-astronomers) and the scepter accompanied by a shield. The scepter, commonly called *manikin*, takes the form of a small figure with a long, curved nose, and with one leg that ends in a serpent's head. This object, held in the right hand of the person being depicted, and the shield, held in the left, were probably the insignia of civil or state power. With the earliest group of stelae in Quiriguá, a change occurs in the function of the sculpted figures. The figure in Stele S (dated 746) bears a scepter, and the figure in Stele H (751) is probably a priest with a ceremonial stick. In the stele dated 756, however, the personage who follows the priest holds both the scepter and the shield. A subsequent example, Stele F, dated 761, also has two personages — with the figures on the front bearing a ceremonial

Quiriguá: Stele F, dated 9.16.10.0.0., or I Ahau 8 Zip (A.D. 761). Height: almost twenty-four feet. The numbers of the hieroglyphic inscription are represented by variants in the forms of heads, or "cephalomorphic glyphs."

Quiriguá: Stele D, dated 9.16.15.0.0. or 7 Ahau 18 Pop (A.D. 766). Height: twenty feet. This detail of the first six glyphs in the "initial series," which give the erection date of the monument, depicts whole human figures. Complex dating signs such as these are very rare.

stick and the figure on the back holding both scepter and shield. Other dignitaries of the city also appear to be depicted, but here the religious representative seems to occupy a privileged place.

The stelae of the following period — Stele D (766) and the famous Stele E (771) — represent still another change, this time a radical one. On these stelae, the two faces of the monoliths contain only personages with both scepter and shield, depicting what are believed to be civil dignitaries. What may have been the prevalence of civil power does not seem to last long, however. In 775 the twin stelae A and C bear figures with the two-headed ceremonial stick on every side — representing four priests. It is also significant that these two monuments mark a temporary suspension of the construction of the tall monoliths that so characterize this age.

Zoomorphic Blocks

In 780 an abrupt change takes place. The traditional stelae now transform into massive rocks representing a fantastic or mythological animal. Archaeologists name these "zoomorphic" blocks.

Block B, which is about seven feet high, fifteen feet long, and eleven feet wide, represents a large monster in a bent position. Its open jaws spew forth a human being's head, arms and torso. The hieroglyphs giving the construction date, 780, depict personages whose entire bodies are visible, a rare occurrence in Mayan art. Blocks G (785) and O (790) — the latter accompanied by a sacrifice and offerings altar — belong to the same family of monsters that spew forth men. The last of the series, Block P, depicts a sumptuously dressed man seated cross-legged in front of the monster's jaws. He holds the scepter and shield. This monument and its related altar were built in 795.

At this point another change occurs: a classical-type stele that marks the following five years (Stele I, thirteen feet high, dated 800), shows a dignitary with scepter and shield on the front side, and a cross-legged figure seated on the back side. The quality of sculpture here is exceptional. Finally, Stele K, signals perhaps a return to a balance of power, with a civil dignitary on one side and a high priest on the other. This monolith, eleven feet high, was built in 805.

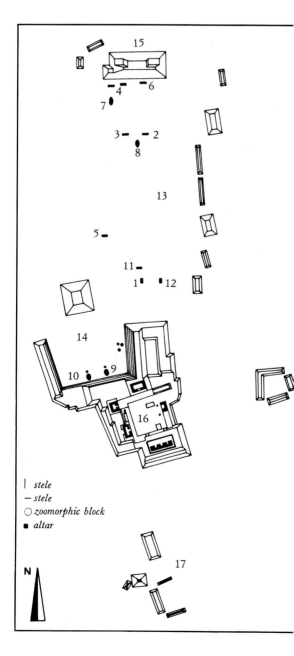

Quiriguá: General plan: (This is the principal nucleus of the Quiriguá monuments. Stelae T and S, mentioned in the text, are not included, as they are situated some distance from this center.)

1. *Stele J*
2. *Stele F.*
3. *Stele E*
4. *Twin stelae A and C*
5. *Stele H*
6. *Stele D*
7. *Zoomorphic block B*
8. *Zoomorphic block G*
9. *Zoomorphic block O*
10. *Zoomorphic block P*
11. *Stele I*
12. *Stele K*
13. *Main plaza*
14. *Ceremonial plaza*
15. *North Group*
16. *Plaza of the Temple*
17. *South Group*

| *stele*
— *stele*
○ *zoomorphic block*
■ *altar*

N

The Notation of Time

The great theme of Maya civilization is the passage of time. Calculations far into the past occur in many hieroglyphic texts, and the text on one of the stele at Quiriguá refers to a date of perhaps ninety million years ago. The construction of each stele mirrored the Maya adoration of time. They were built upon consultation with Mayan calendars, which were of miraculous precision. And although the Maya knew nothing about optics, mechanical clocks, the sandglass, or the water clock — all the instruments that measure periods of time less than a day (hours, minutes, seconds) — the duration of the Mayan solar year was actually more precise than our Gregorian year, as the following figures bear out. The solar year as determined by modern astronomy contains 365.2422 days; the Mayan calendar has 365.2420; and the Gregorian calendar has 365.2425. By means of countless nightly observations the Maya could set the lunation dates. Their Venus calendar, containing 584 days, is also remarkably precise, since modern science states that the duration of the synodical revolution of Venus is 583.920! The Maya carried out such observations and measurements, as the codices tell us, simply with two pieces of crossed wood, on which they placed a long jade tube that helped to concentrate their sight.

The secret of the astronomical achievements of the Maya lies in their ingenuity as well as in the continuity of their observations and their meticulous notations. The Dresden Codex, one of the three authentic Mayan texts (described in detail later), contains no less than 405 annotations about lunations, which represent observations over a thirty-three year period. It is certain that other documents, which no longer exist, must have contained the notations of many other star movements observed for hundreds of years. Such an accumulation of carefully observed and methodically catalogued astronomical data induced the Mayan astronomers to establish a means of making corrections in their solar, lunar, and Venus calendars, thus giving them extraordinary precision.

The dates on the Mayan stelae are not represented by solar, lunar or Venus years, but by the number of days that have passed from a specific chronological starting point, known as *baktun 13*, apparently established in the distant past, because its transcription dates back to 3113 B.C. In

Quiriguá: Zoomorphic Block B, dated
9.17.10.0.0., or 12 Ahau 8 Pax (A.D. 780).
Height: seven feet. Length: fifteen feet.
Width: eleven feet. A human head emerges
from the jaws of a monster.

order to measure and notate the days, the Maya invented a numbers system in which one point represents one unit, and a line represents five units. For large calculations they invented a system of position, using the zero. Their calculating system was based on the number twenty; that is, they counted by twenties, and their numerical progression went from low to high. This means that any movement of a number — a point, a line or a combination of the two — upwards (or +1 point), automatically multiplied the number by twenty. Thus a point at the lowest end of twenty-system scale is worth one unit, and a line is worth five units. On the next level, then, the point becomes $1 \times 20 = 20$ and the line is $5 \times 20 = 100$. Continuing up further, one point means $1 \times 20 \times 20 = 400$, and the line becomes $5 \times 20 \times 20 = 2,000$. And so on.

In order to calculate time based on the solar year, the Mayan priest-astronomers modified the value of the twenty-system scale slightly, but only as regards the notation of the dates. Every level bears a particular name and is identified by a special glyph. Thus we have the following system:

+1 point equals $1 \times 20 \times 18 \times 20 \times 20 = 144{,}000$ days, or 400 numerical years, or one *baktun*.

+1 point equals $1 \times 20 \times 18 \times 20 = 7{,}200$ days, or 20 numerical years, or one *katun*.

+1 point equals $1 \times 20 \times 18 = 360$ days, or one numerical year, or one *tun*.

+1 point equals $1 \times 20 = 20$ days, or one month, or one *uinal*.

+1 point equals one day, or one *kin*.

As stated earlier, the Maya erected a stele at the end of every *katun*, that is to say every 20 years, and sometimes at the end of every *hotun* (5 years) — with numerical years containing 360 days. This rather conventional system of calculating past time was adopted by the Maya of the classical period in order to record the date of the construction of their monuments, and is indicated by the terms "long count" or "initial series." This twenty-system mathematical progression was unlimited and embraced all possible calculations; but it seems that the notations of time inscribed on the monuments generally do not go beyond the *baktun*, the Mayan century, at least as regards multiplication. (The "short count," a simplified version of this counting system was used in the post-classic era. It will be described in a later chapter.)

Various sources, above all the calculations and computations in reverse, do indicate that the chronological starting point of the Maya was *baktun 13*. Such a remote date might have commemorated a mythical event — the creation of the world, for example — or might have had some esoteric meaning. It is interesting that this strange *baktun 13* is represented in an unusual manner at Quiriguá, at the top of the hieroglyphic inscription on the eastern face of Stele C.

The Mayan hieroglyphs characteristically bear two forms for the same subject: either a geometric abstraction, which is the most common, or the head of a god, man or animal. The numbers, generally represented by points and lines, can also appear in the form of a glyph, depicting the head of the god of the number concerned. This notation is rare, but it is found at Quiriguá on Stelae J and F. As for the units of time, a *kin*, a *uinal*, a *tun*, or a *katun* are all represented by symbolic glyphs called "cephalomorphic" glyphs. On Stele D, and on zoomorphic block B and the altar of Block O, the glyphs for time units depict the entire bodies of animals or humans. Once again Quiriguá distinguishes itself by its exceptions.

Structure I

Structure I, the last dated monument at Quiriguá, must have been a splendid edifice. It was built in A.D. 810 northeast of the city, and this date marks the end of the *katun*. After this great architectural complex, the people of Quiriguá did not build any more stelae, monuments or temples, and the city apparently was deserted by its inhabitants. Situated in one of the most fertile zones in Mayan territory, it seems to have been the first Mayan city to experience this phenomenon. In spite of the many hypotheses put forward by archaeologists and scholars, the problem of how and why the Mayan ritual centers were abandoned remains unsolved.

Seibal

In the context of other Mayan sites, Seibal, in Petén, presents few singular characteristics. Its ruins rise above the right bank of the Rio de la Pasión, a tributary of the Usumacinta River in Guatemala. Soon after it was discovered, the Guatemalan government sent an expedition to explore it (1892). Teobert Maler, a Harvard University archaeologist, visited the site in 1895 and 1905, and another American authority, Sylvanus G. Morley, observed the site soon after.

Seibal was apparently one of the latest classical Mayan centers to be established, and archaeological evidence indicates that it may have been influenced by the Toltecs (a central Mexican population.) While the personages sculpted on the stelae wear the common Mayan dress, the figures also reflect Toltec characteristics. Both the gods and the motifs represented, such as the serpent and the speech-scroll, can be identified with central Mexico rather than the classical Mayan culture.

Archaeologists from Harvard University have been excavating Seibal since 1961, and although definitive accounts of these diggings are not yet available, a series of brief published articles relate some of their discoveries: thus, on Stele 19 a figure bears a mask of the Toltec god of wind, Ehecatl; and the volutes on Stele 13 are Toltec symbols for "word." The researchers have also found samples of Toltec pottery and the platform of a circular temple on the site — the only structure of its kind in Petén. But the true significance of Seibal emerges only when it is placed in the total context of the development of the classical Mayan centers.

Other Classical Sites

The development of the classical Mayan civilization in the highlands and lowlands of Guatemala and southern Mexico (Chiapas) continued unabated for several centuries, apparently, with ceremonial centers springing up in different areas. From about A.D. 292 to 435 Tikal was probably the chief cultural center, extending its influence to the neighboring sites of Uaxactún, Balakbal, and Oalan, each of which have dated stelae, altars, temples, and other signs of the classical Maya civilization. From approximately 435 to 534, it seems that the culture spread to sites such as Copán, Cerro de Las Mesas, Altar de Sacrificios, Piedras Negras, Yaxchilán, Palenque, and others. Other sites that began to flourish during this time were Tulúm, Pusilhá, Yaxhá, Uxul, Naranjo, and Cobá. (While the exact dating of each site is always open to subsequent investigations, the establishment of some chronological order has been necessary for the study of the Maya.)

Archaeological evidence indicates a lessening of activity during the early part of the seventh century — revealed by a lack of stelae and other typical monuments. A "renaissance" then occurred, however, between the eighth and ninth centuries, forming a sort of golden age of the Maya civilization. About twenty new cities sprang up about this time, among them Seibal and Nakum, and several of the older sites experienced a revival of architectural and artistic endeavors. The earliest date inscribed on the step of a structure at Seibal corresponds to A.D. 750, and the latest date recorded at this site is 869 — indicating that Seibal was one of the last Maya centers in this area to be deserted.

Seibal: Stele 10, dated 10.1.0.0.0. (A.D. 849). Although the figure in this stele has all the attributes of a Mayan king-priest, he is also distinguished by Toltec characteristics (among them the small jade stick inserted through his nose.)

THE CREATION OF MANKIND

When they made man, they fashioned him of earth, and they fed him with wood, they fed him with leaves. They wished that only earth should enter into his making. But he did not talk, he did not walk, he had neither blood nor flesh, so our early fathers and grandfathers told us, oh, my sons! They did not know what should enter into the man. But at length they found whereof to make it. Only two animals knew that there was food in Paxil, the place where those animals are found which are called the Coyote and the Crow. The Coyote animal was killed, and in his remains, when he was quartered, corn was discovered. And the animal called Tiuh-tiuh, searching for the dough of the corn, brought from out of the sea the blood of the tapir and the serpent, and with it the maize was kneaded. With this dough the flesh of man was made by the Creator and the Maker. Thus the Creator, the Maker, the Progenitors knew how to make man complete, so they tell. Man having been made, there resulted thirteen males and fourteen females; there was one woman extra.

Then they talked, they had blood, they had flesh. They married and multiplied. One of them had two wives. Thus they mated, so the old people used to say, oh, our sons! They had daughters, they had sons, those first men. Thus was the creation of man. So the Obsidian Stone was made.

The Annals of the Cakchiquels
(pp. 46–47)

DOS POZOS

The 1960 discovery of Dos Pozos, southeast of Lake Petexbatum in a heavily forested region of Petén, followed the pattern of the discovery of many Mayan cities. Several such discoveries have been curiously linked with the gathering of the secretion of the big sapodillas, or tropical evergreen trees, whose white latex contains chicle — used to produce chewing gum. Deserted from the tenth century on by the Mayas, the immense forests of Petén began to be frequented about a hundred years ago by a handful of "chicleros," or chicle harvesters who make annual expeditions to find and cut the chicle trees. During their work they sometimes discover archaeological sites, and when they return home they notify the local or provincial authorities.

It is of more than passing interest to note that the cradle of Mayan civilization is also that of the sapodilla. An imaginary map indicating the spread of this tree would actually correspond to the territory occupied by the Maya during their classical period. The chicle tree was always one of the Maya's great allies. At Tikal splendid panels made of sapodilla wood have resisted a thousand years of bad weather and have withstood the pressure of stone bricks in a rather precarious state of balance. Also, numerous Mayan constructions contain old supporting beams made of sapodilla wood. Moreover, the latex, mixed with a second resin of the region, supplies an incense that was highly prized by the Mayas in their religious ceremonies — as valuable as copal. Without a doubt the sapodilla tree, like the cocoa plant whose wild species (*Theobrama bicolor*) also originates in Petén, played an important part in the lives of the Mayas.

In the area where Dos Pozos was discovered, the sapodillas produce a latex secretion of inferior quality, and for this reason the chicleros never ventured there. It was not until 1960 that an expedition (led by this author) found the ruins of an ancient Mayan city in the area, naming it for the two deep wells found on the premises. (The site has also come to be known locally as Dos Pilas, or "two stelae.") Later in the 1960s, a young English scholar, Ian Graham, confirmed the fact that Mayas had settled in this area when he authenticated and catalogued the vestiges of another Mayan site, La Aguateca, relatively near Dos Pozos. A third nearby site, El Tamarindo, has been found by an American geologist on a petroleum prospecting campaign. According to Ian Graham, who continues to identify, classify, and catalogue the data of the Petexbatun River region, Dos Pozos was the center of the Mayan culture in the area, and its influence can be seen in the hieroglyphs at La Aguateca.

The architectural peculiarity of Dos Pozos seems to have been its unfinished stairway. Rather than a typical four-step sculpted stairway, this example contains only three steps; the fourth, smooth and bearing no inscriptions, was found lying nearby. Even the third step, set firmly in place, bears traces of sculpting that was not completed: on the left, the hieroglyphs are barely sketched, and on the right, only their disposition is traced. On the central stones of the steps, bas-relief sculptures depict court scenes; these scenes stand out, but the heads of the personages are disfigured. There is no doubt that this stone stairway was abandoned during construction and then systematically mutilated by vandals.

The true significance of Dos Pozos is that, for the first time in the history of Mayan archaeology, there is tangible proof of the sudden desertion of a classical city. If all the ghost cities of the Petén had shown such evident traces of a drastic interruption of work in progress (if not actual mutilation), scholars could advance the hypothesis of a warring invasion as the cause of the fall of the classical Mayan civilization. But the evidence at Dos Pozos is unique, and is not enough to support or prove such a theory. It indicates internal struggles or a foreign invasion involving only the Dos Pozos area. Future systematic excavations, or perhaps an analagous discovery, might present different explanations for the end of the classic Mayan world in Petén.

Dos Pozos: A sculpted panel seven feet high, which is set halfway up the main pyramid of the site. It depicts a king-priest wearing the traditional dress reserved for the rites of sacrificing one's own blood.

THE MIGRATION OF THE TRIBES

Then we arrived at the shore of the sea. There all the tribes and the warriors were reunited at the shore of the sea. And when they looked upon it, their hearts were heavy.

"There is no way to cross it; we know of no one who has crossed the sea," the warriors and the seven tribes said to each other. "Who has a log on which we can cross, our brother? We trust only in you," they all said. And we spoke to them in this manner: "Go, you, go first, carefully." "How can we cross in truth, we who are here?" Thus we all said. Thus they said: "Have pity on us, oh, brother! who have come to gather here on the shore of the sea, unable to see our mountains and our valleys. If we remain here to sleep, we shall be conquered, we the two eldest sons, the chiefs and heads, the first warriors of the seven tribes, oh, our brother! Would that we could cross and see without delay the gifts which our mothers and our fathers have given us, oh, my brother!" Thus they talked with each other, those who engendered the Quichés. And our grandfathers Gagavitz and Zactecauh said: "We say to you: Let us go to work, our brothers! We have not come to stay here huddled at the shore of the sea, without being able to look upon our country which we were told we should see, you our warriors, our seven tribes. Let us plunge into the sea immediately!" Thus they said, and at once all of them were filled with joy.

"When we arrived at the gates of Tulán, we received a red stick which was our staff, and because of that we were given the name of Cakchiquels, oh, our sons!" said Gagavitz and Zactecauh. "Let us thrust the points of our staffs in the sand under the sea and we shall soon cross the sea on the sand, using the red sticks which we went to receive at the gates of Tulán." Thus we passed, over the rows of sand, when it widened below the sea and on the surface of the sea. Immediately all were rejoiced when they saw the sands below the sea. Thereupon they held counsel. "There is our hope, there on the first land we must be reunited," they said, "only there can we be organized now that we have arrived from Tulán."

They plunged forward then and passed over the sand; those who came at the rear entered the sea as we emerged from the waters on the other bank. Afterwards the seven tribes became fearful, then all the warriors spoke and the seven tribes said: "Have you not seen our gifts? Have we not humbled ourselves before you, oh, lords! oh, warriors! Did we not come with you to the east? Have we not come to seek our mountains and our valleys? Have you not seen our gifts, the green feathers, the blue feathers, the garlands?" Thus spoke the seven tribes united in counsel. And saying, "It is well," the seven tribes ended their conference.

The Annals of the Cakchiquels
(pp. 54–56)

The Fate of the Classical Maya

Many hypotheses have been put forward to explain the fall and sudden disappearance of the Mayan civilization in this area. Sylvanus G. Morley, when he wrote *The Ancient Maya*, rejected the idea of wars and internal struggles. Rather, he saw the cause of decadence and eventual desertion of the sites in the failure of the Mayan agricultural system. The site of Quiriguá, however, also in Guatemala, lies in a fertile plain of abundant humus and plentiful rainfall, and could have fed thousands of people for centuries. Yet Quiriguá is said to be the first classical Mayan city to have been abandoned.

What of other hypotheses? Earthquakes? No site reveals traces of such a cataclysm. Time, inclement weather, encroaching forests, and the fragility of some materials seem to be responsible for the destruction of many of the monuments. And although earthquakes are frequent and violent on the Guatemalan plateaus, they do not exist in Petén. Ironically, also, the Indians of the plateau have never deserted their land, despite the history of earthquakes.

The theory of a climatic change, advanced after a pluviometric study made in California, was rejected almost as soon as it was offered. It has been demonstrated that an excessive increase of rain would have favored agriculture, while a decrease would not have brought about great changes. Examples of this phenomenon are to be found today in the areas bordering Petén. As for the theory of repeated yellow fever or malaria epidemics, which might have depopulated the Mayan lands, this can be rejected as well. Neither malaria, an Old World disease, nor yellow fever, of African origin, is known to have existed in America before the arrival of the Spanish. Moreover, no epidemic, not even the black plague that devastated Europe, has ever been known to cause the downfall of an entire civilization. Then again, it would seem impossible to localize an epidemic to the region of Petén only, and not touching neighboring areas.

Through my discoveries at Dos Pozos, I have arrived at what I believe to be a plausible explanation for the disappearance of the Maya in a study of the phenomenon that oriented and dominated the life of the classical Maya: time. My hypothesis, set forth at length in the work, *Découvertes chez les Maya*, (*Discoveries in the Home of the Maya*), runs as follows. Elaborating a monstrous, complex calendar in order to imprison time, the Mayan priest-astronomers probably thought they possessed the key to the universe. They had the intoxicating impression of being the masters of the world. They imposed the laws of time on the social organization of their society — creating arithmetic, the arts, astronomy, and writing — all in order to serve time better. These were the sciences reserved for an elite, however, which strengthened their power. And as I see it, this became a case of "sorcerers" being the victims themselves.

In the tenth century the priest-astronomers announced the coming end of the fourth world, and hence the end of the human race. The problem was that, as legends and writings of the Yucatán Indians record, the ancestors of the present-day Mayas believed that they lived in the "fourth" world, which was destined to disappear . . . in order to bring about a fifth world where no men lived. Evidence of these beliefs can be found in oral traditions as well.

By reconstructing the workings of the Mayan calendars, it has been established that the last temporal sequence of the fourth world, heralding the end of the human race, corresponded to the tenth century — the very century that the Mayas deserted their cities. Escaping from the land where they had lived for so many centuries, leaving their temples and monuments, the Maya might have enacted a sort of voluntary, artificial "judgment day." In this way they may have subjected themselves to the annihilation predicted by their extraordinary calculation of time.

Dos Pozos: This unfinished stairway, which has only three sculptured steps, testifies to an apparently abrupt interruption of architectural activity in this city.

Dos Pozos: Detail from Stele 2, dated 9.15.
4.6.4, or 8 Kan, 17 Muan (A.D. 736). The
signs in front of the mouth of this figure suggest the word, or song, a rare symbol in
Mayan iconography.

Yaxchilán

The Usumacinta, the largest river in Central America, begins at the confluence of the Río de la Pasión and the Chixoy, which flow down from the mountains of Guatemala. For centuries, waters of the Usumacinta have gnawed at the outskirts of Yaxchilán, in the Chiapas region of Mexico. Yaxchilán is practically inaccessible, and neither excavation nor significant research has been carried out on the site. Along the river, a series of rapids render navigation dangerous, and the trek overland through the forest is tedious.

The site of Yaxchilán was probably known for a long time earlier, but it became known officially in the 1880s when the Englishman Alfred Maudslay carried out scientific observations there. He was the first to explore the ruins carefully, drawing accurate plans, taking photographs, and copying hieroglyphic inscriptions and sculpture designs. He christened the site *Menche*, the Mayan word for "green tree." A second visitor, Désiré Charnay, called the site *Lorillard*, after the American patron of his expedition; and a few years later the Austrian-born archaeologist Teobert Maler, who represented the Peabody Museum of Harvard for many years, gave it its third and definitive name, Yaxchilán, which means "place of the green stones." Oddly enough, however, Yaxchilán does not have the look of a river town, because the edifices do not overlook or dominate the river.

The ruins of Yaxchilán are all but lost in the forest, and it is necessary to consult a map of the site in order to understand the complex and to reach the eighty-six numbered edifices. Some lie on the hill near the edge of the river, but are set apart from it; others rest on the first elevated parts of the land, parallel to the former structures. Still others were constructed on elevations of land farther into the forest. None of these structures present any outstanding architectural features, as compared to some of the structures on other Mayan sites.

As stated earlier in the text, the origin of the Mayan temple was a simple hut; it was an image of a sanctuary, but resembled a family hut with its conical roof. Over the centuries the image became a stone building, although the use of heavy stone (particularly in constructing vaults and "arches") greatly limited the interior space. The rooms of the temple became dark and narrow so that the stone walls could support the weight of the structure. (It is interesting to note that the Mayan word *actun* signifies both "temple" and "cavern.") In effect, the interior of the Mayan temple does represent a sort of cavern — the heart of a people's religious activity, magic rites, and secrets. Even among today's descendants of the Maya, a cavern holds a privileged place and is invested with significant symbolism.

Structure 33 is perhaps the most interesting at Yaxchilán. It rises from a small hill and belongs to the architectural group that has been christened the "Great Acropolis." A series of small stairways lead to the building, which is almost completely enveloped in vegetation. Three portals open out from the facade, and a tiled "roof comb," a sort of perforated brick gable as high as the edifice itself, crowns the roof above the central wall. This superstructure — typical of Mayan architecture — is essentially decorative, balancing the proportions of the building and setting it in relief. At one time, an eight-foot statue belonged in the central niche of this roof comb, but today it is gone. This was presumably an important figure with a headdress of feathers. Three other niches above the portals also must have housed statues of important persons, seated cross-legged on seats in the form of a serpent.

A life-size stone statue of a decapitated man sits in front of the main portal. This figure (called *Atsbilán* — "he who sets the sun") was "still alive" in the hearts of the inhabitants of this forest until just a few years ago; about one hundred long-haired Lacandón Indians, who wear long tunics, frequented this deserted temple until only recently to celebrate magical religious rites.

Yaxchilán: Structure 33: Plan and schematic drawing.

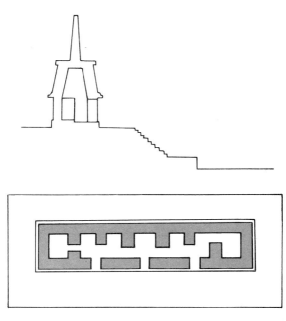

Yaxchilán: General plan
1. Usumacinta River   5. Structure 33
2. Great Plaza   6. Minor pyramids
3. Sacred Ball Court   7. Capitol
4. Great Acropolis

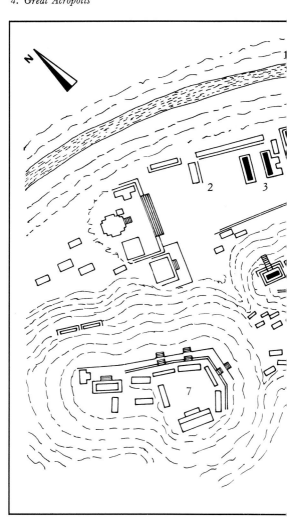

The unusual features of Yaxchilán are the sculpted stone panels or lintels under the temple entrances. There are fifty-eight of these masterpieces in the area, while there are only thirty typical stelae and sixteen altars. The lintels, which are ornamented with beautifully carved figures in stucco and stone, can be divided into two series: scenes of social life and scenes of religious activity. The former almost always contain two persons, who have long, deformed heads and noses modeled according to the Mayan ideal of beauty. The taller person appears to be the more important: his face is in profile, his body faces forward, and his heels are together with his feet pointing outward. The second man, much shorter, is entirely in profile. Both figures wear similar sumptuous clothes, and they both hold a ceremonial stick: a cross decorated with feathers or flowers, and a miniature of the large-nosed god. Since the two figures are alike, they probably have the same title, and it can be surmised that these scenes represent a phase in the transfer of power from one person to another (an event that probably took place every twenty years, or *katun*.)

Initiation rites, ecstatic practices, and visions appear to be portrayed on the bas-reliefs of the second series of lintels. On Number 26, for

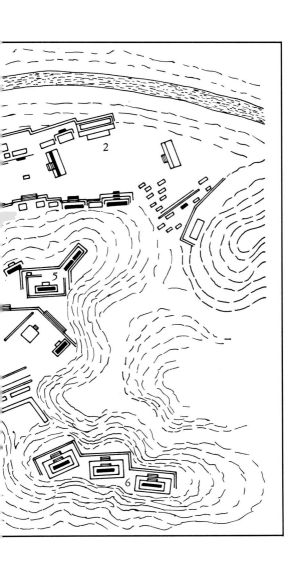

Yaxchilán: Another detail from Lintel 26. This personage, whose face is marked with scars, was probably a priest of the "Jaguar" order, as he holds a jaguar head in his hands. (National Museum of Anthropology, Mexico City)

example, a neophyte receives from the high priest a jaguar head or mask. Lintels that depict voluntary sacrifices show magnificently dressed men piercing their tongues with a thorned cord and then passing the cord through the hole; their blood falls into a basket full of copal and rubber incense sticks.

City-State Relationships

The Mayan sites during the classical period were apparently grouped in autonomous city-states, and it appears from a study of glyphs and archaeological styles that Yaxchilán had some influence over the neighboring site of Bonampak (described in a subsequent chapter.) The so-called "emblem glyph" of Yaxchilán (a particular glyph archaeologists associate with this site) is represented also at Bonampak, and many of the sculptural details at Yaxchilán appear to have affected development at Bonampak. Nothing else is yet known that would verify when this might have taken place; all we know is that the Yaxchilán-Bonampak culture was active until approximately A.D. 810.

Palenque

Of all the Mayan cities of the classical period, Palenque, in the Chiapas region of Mexico, is perhaps the most famous, the most accessible, and the most visited. In 1750 a group of Spanish adventurers found the site and gave it the local name of Casas de Piedras, or "houses of stone." Don José Calderon and the Italian architect Antonio Bernasconi, who visited the region and wrote a report in 1784, were precursors of later travelers who would take the first, uncertain steps to explore these ancient monuments. In 1787, Captain Antonio de Rio, sent by the King of Spain to explore the region, named the site after a neighboring village: Palenque. Certain "investigations" followed, whose techniques would horrify modern archaeologists. (A report based on these studies, published much later in Europe in 1882, was accompanied by the comments of Paul F. Cabrera, who wanted to demonstrate that the city's populace was of Egyptian origin.)

From the early nineteenth century on, Palenque became an obligatory stop for anyone interested in pre-Columbian civilizations. In 1807 G. Dupaix carried out a survey of the site, and his report was published accompanied by many interesting drawings by Castaneda. The French artist Frédéric de Waldeck, who was known to "reconstruct" ruins as he drew them, spent two years at Palenque (1832-34) and believed he saw elephant heads in the hieroglyphic inscriptions. This was a purely subjective and erroneous vision, which he reproduced in his drawings (published in 1866) with such realism that any attempt to establish the age of Palenque became completely bogged down. Since elephants had disappeared from the American continent many millennia before, the birth of the city was thought for a while to have taken place in a most distant past. (Despite the mistakes and often blind enthusiasm of early archaeological explorers, however, their drawings afford an inexhaustible source of information, and the accounts that accompany them reflect the mood of an entire age.)

John L. Stephens visited Palenque in 1839. In his work, *Incidents of Travel in Central America, Chiapas and Yucatán*, magnificently illustrated by Frederick Catherwood, Stephens described Palenque in a scintillating style, and analyzed the historical sources of the enigmatic culture of its constructors. Thanks to the seriousness of his observations, he succeeded in giving an objective picture of Palenque without neglecting the near miraculous aspect of the town and its discovery.

When in 1857 Désiré Charnay visited Palenque, he did not find evidence of Egyptian or Carthaginian civilizations, but suggestions of a Toltec influence. At last the archaeological remains of Indian America were placed in their American context. Finally in 1889, the Englishman Alfred Maudslay published a map of Palenque and a purely objective description of the site.

Palenque: From left to right — the Temple of the Cross, the Temple of the Hill, and the Temple of the Sun. Each was built in A.D. 692.

The Art of Stucco

The road to Palenque arrives from the west, and just as in Yaxchilán the edifices follow the topography of the area. The Palace comes into view first, and then, to the right, the Temple of the Inscriptions. Various little temples lie to the east, among them the Temples of the Cross, the Sun, and the Foliated Cross, barely visible through the surrounding vegetation. To the north of the Palace rises a series of

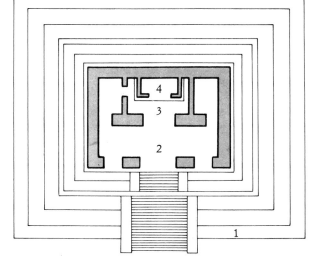

Palenque: Plan of the Temple of the Sun.
1. *Pyramid*
2. *First chamber*
3. *Second chamber*
4. *Small temple containing the bas-relief of the Sun.*

edifices, the North Group, which includes the Temple of the Count. A pre-Columbian aqueduct directs the waters of the Otulun, a stream, to the center of the city: the only example of this type of construction in Mayan civilization.

The flat and swampy land of the Tabasco region ends at Palenque, on the first mountainous spurs of northern Chiapas. A slow infiltration of water into the area has been fortunate, however, because it has coated many of Palenque's admirable stucco reliefs with a protective

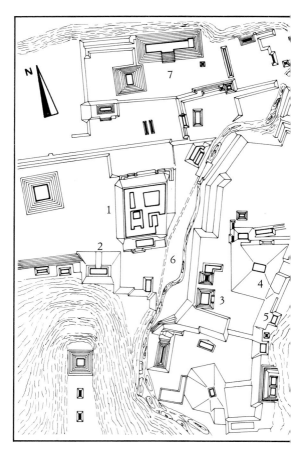

Palenque: General plan.
1. The Palace
2. The Pyramid and the Temple of the Inscriptions
3. Temple of the Sun
4. Temple of the Cross
5. Temple of the Foliated Cross
6. Aqueduct
7. North Group

layer of limestone. Penetrating the blanket of humid heat that suffocates the countryside, the visitor must bear in mind that Palenque is the capital of stucco. All the classical period Mayan buildings were covered with stucco-work, but it is rare to admire it *in situ* today, owing to the extreme fragility of this material. By using a fine-grained lime with a water and resin mixture, the Maya obtained a stucco that hardened as it dried. Once exposed to the humidity, however, it tended to alter. At Palenque some of the stucco reliefs escaped this fate for hundreds of years until the cutting down of trees (in order to excavate and open the reliefs to full view) upset the hygrometric balance of the area. In recent years, unfortunately, numerous decorations have turned to dust. The amount of stucco work left on the facades can allow one to imagine what the whole must have been like — but for many of the details, scholars must now turn to the drawings of Castaneda, Waldeck, and Catherwood, who saw them before they were damaged.

The unparalleled quality of these reliefs has been the greatest contributing factor to Palenque's fame. The specimens of decorative stucco work remaining in other Mayan cities does not reach the exceptional artistic qualities of these sculptures.

The Temple of the Sun

In the last century, however, Palenque was most noted for other reasons. At that time it owed its fame to three magnificent bas-reliefs,

Palenque: Detail from the stone reliquary in
the Temple of the Foliated Cross. The bas-
relief depicts a priest holding a "manikin,"
symbol of power.

On the following pages:
Palenque: Panorama of the city. In the foreground, left, Temple of the Sun; to the far
right, Temple of the Foliated Cross (A.D. 692).
Elegant tiled and perforated gables ("roof
combs") surmount each temple. The large
Palace with its square tower can be seen in
the center.

those of the Sun, the Cross, and the Foliated Cross. These bas-reliefs
were used in naming the three identical temples that house them —
temples that are set on the heights east of the Palace. In no other
Mayan construction does one find such a masterly distribution of
volume as in these architectural "jewels." Simple, graceful, and
balanced, with their roof combs made of two inclining strata, these
three temples give the impression of lightness, although they are built
of enormous blocks. In fact, the volume of their interiors is less than
the volume of the materials enclosing them. (Although in Palenque the
walls are thinner than in any other classical period temples.)

The structure of the Temple of the Sun varies from that of the other
two temples. This temple, set on a twenty-six foot pyramid, has five
stories. Including the fourteen-foot roof comb, it reaches a height of
almost forty feet. Two parallel halls, each ten feet wide, divide the
structure, with a stairway on the eastern facade leading to the first
hall. There, three doors are set in a thick, three-foot-wide wall.

The temples must have been fascinating when the colors of the stucco design were still preserved. It is still possible to discern, over the entrance, fragments of the stucco frieze that once decorated the upper portion of the slightly inclined facade. At the center of the frieze is a crouching figure, surrounded by masks and serpents; two other crouching figures decorate the corners. Below this, dignitaries with feathered headdresses cover the central bands of the facade. Large hieroglyphs cover the two corner bands.

To the left and right of the main entrance to the Temple of the Sun, two life-sized clothed figures are sculpted in stone. Inside the first hall, a large opening in the central wall leads into the second main hall. There, set against the back wall is an almost cubical construction which must have served as a sanctuary — a secret temple with nothing more than a tiny opening through which a ray of light penetrates.

Further on, one of the masterpieces of Mayan art appears (along with Palenque's bas-reliefs of the Cross and the Foliated Cross) — the bas-relief of the Sun. Ten feet wide and three-and-a-half feet high,

Palenque: View of the edifices that look on to the eastern courtyard of the Palace, the largest structure in this architectural complex. A parapet decorated with bas-reliefs and interrupted by stairs surrounds the courtyard.

this work is almost invisible — covered as it is with moss and immersed in half-light. Only with the aid of artificial light can the visitor discern the details of this precious relic of fine limestone. The subject, which is similar to scenes in the lintels in Yaxchilán, depicts two personages, one in front of the other, exchanging a tiny figure of the long-nosed god. The person on the left is shorter. Both are standing erect on the backs of two prostrate men, probably slaves; between the two main figures, two other seated slaves hold a highly decorated ceremonial stick; the slaves appear to bend under the weight of the burden. Above this altar, two crossed lances hold up a shield decorated with a mask of the sun god. Four lines of hieroglyphs extend over the backs of the principal figures.

The Bas-reliefs of the Cross and of the Foliated Cross

The bas-relief of the Cross, found in the temple bearing the same name, has provoked a great deal of written comment because of the

monumental cross sculpted in the center. Dupaix and his commentators were the first to emphasize the fact that this symbol was frequently used before the advent of Christianity, and its presence in this place perhaps demonstrated the antiquity of the temple that housed it. As for the Catholic priests of the Palenque region, after Stephens's restoration of the bas-relief, they suddenly decided (arbitrarily) that it dated from the third century A.D. and that the ancient inhabitants of the region had been Christian! They could not know, of course, at a time when nothing was known of pre-Columbian culture, that the cross was a fundamental symbol of the Maya, the image of their quadripartite ("four worlds") universe, and the reflection of their world supposedly enclosed between the four cardinal points.

The bas-relief of the Cross, like the other two works of the nearby temples, is composed of three panels, and develops the same theme of the central emblem sculpted between two officials. Only the left panel was still in place when Stephens visited Palenque in 1839. But after searching the area he did find some fragments of the right panel, bearing hieroglyphs, and on the bank of the Otulun River discovered the central panel, which contained the "great personage" and the cross. Exposed to the elements, the sculpted face was covered with mud and rubble. (An inhabitant of the village of Palenque had found it years before and had made plans to use it in decorating his home.

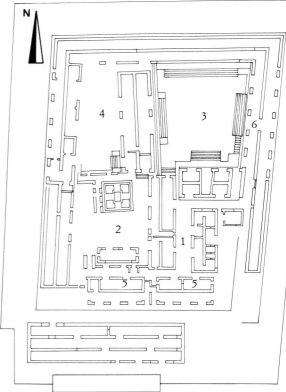

Palenque: The stone panel from the base of western edifice, or Edifice C. Two personages sculpted in profile frame a series of glyphs.

Since he had no means of lifting and transporting the panel, the moving process was difficult and slow — not only because the villager lacked appropriate means, but also because the Mexican government had forbidden the removal of pre-Columbian objects from their sites. Therefore, the bas-relief of the Cross never reached its destination; rather, it had been broken to pieces due to the archaic method of transport, and was abandoned on the stream bank.)

How many other works of art have been lost? It is not known. But some of those that did reach the homes of villagers were found and restored. In one home Stephens found two other sculpted panels; these, according to Dupaix's drawings, originally framed the entrance to the Temple of the Sun sanctuary. The owners of the house, two sisters, were attached to "their" bas-reliefs and jealously looked after their preservation. Getting their authorization to reproduce the bas-reliefs in his notebooks was quite an achievement on Catherwood's part. Today, thanks to the Mexican National Institute of Anthropology and History, a visitor can admire *in situ* a great number of restored masterpieces from Palenque.

The bas-relief of the Foliated Cross is worthy of attention because of its composition and the refinement of its sculpture. Here the smaller personage, usually placed on the left, is on the right. Maize leaves decorate the two horizontal limbs of the cross, which bear on their ends the tiny head of an individual who perhaps symbolizes an ear or grain of maize. A strange bird perches on the top of the Foliated Cross. He wears a mask, and according to the tradition of the Yucatán Maya is the mythical bird Moan.

The Palace

The "Palacio" at Palenque, or Palace, is a group of edifices set on a long trapezoidal platform, which is now reduced to massive ruins. Six columns six feet thick frame the five entrances on the western facade. These columns are remarkable for their stucco figures, which for the most part have resisted centuries of tropical rains.

The mass of constructions that constitute the Palace include dark, dank structures, many badly-aired halls and rooms, and a series of underground storerooms. Among some of the more interesting aspects of the Palace are the narrow dormers in the shape of a T, symbol of the rain god, that line various walls. These were at one time considered Greek crosses and even Egyptian symbols.

The edifices of the Palace border four internal courtyards, much like patios, that have rough, uneven surfaces. The eastern courtyard, the largest, is lovely because of its sculpted stone panels (between the five-step stairways) depicting groups of people. Glyphs appear at regular intervals on the parapet that surrounds the courtyard. In one of the rooms in Edifice A, which faces this courtyard, archaeologists discovered in 1949 a surprising stone slab (7.8 × 8.4 feet) sculpted with 262 glyphs of an extraordinary style. To the left, the first seven glyphs are actually tiny pictures. As in the case of the Quiriguá site, they represent whole figures of men and animals, which is a rare occurrence in Mayan art. The date of these glyphs corresponds to A.D. 672.

The most surprising structure in this architectural complex is the Tower, rising elegantly to a height of forty-nine feet. Its form is unique and is not to be found in any other Mayan city. Fortunately the drawings and descriptions of the nineteenth century visitors to the site confirm the authenticity of the strange structure, which appears "deformed." Stephens was very enthusiastic about its technical details but soon abandoned it, quite disillusioned, as if it had been a trick mirror. The truth is that the exterior does not indicate what the Tower is in reality. The edifice is square, and has three stories each eight feet

Schematic drawing and plan of the Tower.

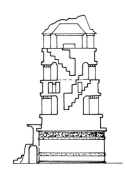

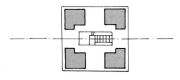

Left:
Palenque: Plan of the Palace.
1. *Central Courtyard*
2. *Courtyard of the Tower*
3. *Eastern Courtyard*
4. *Western Courtyard*
5. *Southern edifices*
6. *Edifice A*

high separated by cornices. However, the monument stands only because of its central nucleus — an enormous inner quadrangular column made of solid cement. Is this a tower, then? Rather, it is a perforated cement block that merely gives the illusion of technical prowess.

The Tower rests on a base twenty-three feet long and thirteen feet high whose northern, eastern and western sides are decorated with nine small seated figures. On the southern side, dignitaries in two sculpted stone panels seem to be brandishing standards. Inside this strange edifice there is no access to the first story. To compensate, there is a very narrow stairway in the central column, which leads to the second and third stories. The interior space of this "tower" is thus a mere narrow corridor that goes around the central column. There appears to be nothing that defines the function of the structure. It could be that the Palenque Tower, like the temples, is a clever replica of primitive wood constructions. Or, it could have been a building meant for astronomical observations.

The Temple of Inscriptions

There is nothing in this sober, classical edifice to indicate that this was the center of an incredible archaeological adventure in Central America. The temple rests on a fifty-two-foot high pyramid made up of nine successive terraces. On the six pillars that frame the five entrances it is still possible to discern stucco figures who hold between their arms monstrous beings with one foot that ends up being a serpent's body. (This is the same type of figure found in Quiriguá.) On both sides of the principal entrance to the second room of the temple, and on the back wall, a series of panels contain 620 sculpted glyphs. This inscription, the longest in Mayan territory except for the Copán stairway, gives the name to the edifice.

In 1949 Alberto Ruz, director of Mexican excavations at Palenque, noticed six closed-finger holes on a slab of rock set into the floor of the vestibule. He tried to raise it, and saw that it was the entrance to a curving corridor with a stairway blocked by stone and earth — a secret passageway. This discovery marked the beginning of three consecutive years of hard work to methodically clear away the staircase. After having excavated the first twenty-six steps, Ruz noted an abrupt change in the orientation of the landings. First, they descend toward the west; but at the twenty-sixth step down they turn and descend toward the east. One year and twenty-two steps later, the archaeologist found himself facing a brickwork wall at the foot of which lay a deposit of offerings: three clay trays, three shells, eleven jade pieces and a pearl. After opening the wall he discovered a large triangular slab set vertically into the floor. At its base a rudimentary sepulcher enclosed six skeletons, (one of which was a woman).

Not without difficulty, Ruz was able to roll the vertical panel away and uncover the entrance to a large vaulted room twenty-one feet high, thirty feet long and almost ten feet wide. Here, with the aid of a flashlight, the archaeologist discovered an extraordinary procession of nine sculptured dignitaries walking one behind the other in a religious attitude all around the room. Dressed like royalty with their headdresses tipped with precious quetzal feathers, these stucco figures were covered with a layer of limestone. Also, stalactites of every shape and size hung down from the roof. The important personages seemed to be guarding a large elevated stone slab set at the center of the room, at the foot of which were two splendid stucco heads, today considered among the treasures of world art.

On the bas-relief covering this monolith, there was a man poised on a mask that represents either the god of death or of the earth; the man bends his knees and stretches his body backward. He seems

THE RISE OF HUNAC CEEL TO POWER

Cabal Xiu was their priest. Uxmal Chac was their commander; formerly he was their priest.

Then Hapay Can was brought to Chemchan. He was pierced by an arrow when he arrived at the bloody wall there at Uxmal.

Then Chac-xib-chac was despoiled of his insignia. Zac-xib-chac and Ek Yuuan Chac were also despoiled of their insignia. Ix Zacbeliz was the name of the maternal grandmother of the Chacs. Ek Yuuan Chac was their father. Hun Yuuan Chac was their youngest brother; Uooh-puc was his name. There was a glyph written on the palm of his hand. Then a glyph was written below his throat, was also written on the sole of his foot and written within the ball of the thumb of Ah Uooh-puc. The Chacs were not gods. The only true God is our Lord Dios; they worshipped him according to the word and the wisdom of Mayapán.

Ah Kin Coba was their priest there in the fortress of Mayapan. Zulim Chan was at the west gate. Nauat was the guardian of the south gate. Couoh was the guardian of the east gate. Ah Ek was his companion. This was their ruler: Ah Tapay Nok Cauich was the name of their head-chief; Hunac Ceel was the representative of Ah Mex Cuc. Then he demanded one complete Plumeria flower. Then he demanded a white mat. Then he demanded a mantle faced on two sides. Then he demanded a green turkey. Then he demanded a mottled snail. Then he demanded the gourds called homa.

Whereupon they departed and arrived at Ppoole, where the remainder of the Itzá were increased in number; they took the women of Ppole as their mothers. Then they arrived at Ake; there they were born at Ake.

The Book of Chilam Balam of Chumayel
(pp. 64–70)

THE RITUAL OF THE FOUR WORLDQUARTERS

The lord of the people of the south is the first of the men of the Noh family. Ix-Kantacay is the name of the first of the men of the Puch family. They guard nine rivers; they guard nine mountains.

The red flint stone is the stone of the red Mucencab. The red ceiba tree of abundance is his arbor which is set in the east. The red bullet-tree is their tree. The red zapote. . . The red-vine. . . Reddish are their yellow turkeys. Red toasted corn is their corn.

The white flint stone is their stone in the north. The white ceiba tree of abundance is the arbor of the white Mucencab. White-breasted are their turkeys. White Lima-beans are their Lima-beans. White corn is their corn.

The black flint stone is their stone in the west. The black ceiba tree of abundance is their arbor. Black speckled corn is their corn. Black tipped camotes are their camotes. Black wild pigeons are their turkeys. Black akab-chan is their green corn. Black beans are their beans. Black Lima-beans are their Lima-beans.

The yellow flint stone is the stone of the south. The ceiba tree of abundance, the yellow ceiba tree of abundance, is their arbor. The yellow bullet-tree is their tree. Colored like the yellow bullet-tree are their camotes. Colored like the yellow bullet-tree are the wild pigeons which are their turkeys. Yellow green corn is their green corn. Yellow-backed are their beans. . .

11 Ahau was the katun when they carried burdens on their backs. Then the land-surveyor first came; this was Ah Ppizte who measured the leagues. Then there came the chacté shrub for marking the leagues with their walking sticks. Then he came to Uac-hab-nal to pull the weeds along the leagues, when Mizcit Ahau came to sweep clean the leagues, when the land-surveyor came. These were long leagues that he measured.

Then a spokesman was established at the head of the mat.

Ix Noh Uc presides to the east. Ox Tocoymoo presides to the east. Ox Pauah Ek presides to the east. Ah Miz presides to the east.

Batun presides to the north. Ah Puch presides to the north. Balam-na presides to the north. Ake presides to the north.

Iban presides to the west. Ah Chab presides to the west. Ah Tucuch presides to the west.

Ah Yamas presides to the south. Ah Puch presides to the south. Cauich presides to the south. Ah Couoh presides to the south. Ah Puc presides to the south.

The red wild bees are in the east. A large red blossom is their cup. The red Plumeria is their flower.

The white wild bees are in the north. The white pachca is their flower. A large white blossom is their cup.

The black wild bees are in the west. The black laurel flower is their flower. A large black blossom is their cup.

The yellow wild bees are in the south. A large yellow blossom is their cup. . . is their flower.

Palenque: One of the many stucco heads that have made this site famous.

Left:
Palenque: Stucco bas-relief that decorates one of the pillars at the entrance to the Palace. Although deteriorated by weather, this stucco-work displays an artistic perfection unsurpassed in most other Mayan cities.

Palenque: Temple of the Inscriptions: plan and schematic drawing indicating the internal stairway that descends to the crypt. On the landing, at the point where the stairway changes direction, an underground passageway leading to the outside of the pyramid affords light and air.

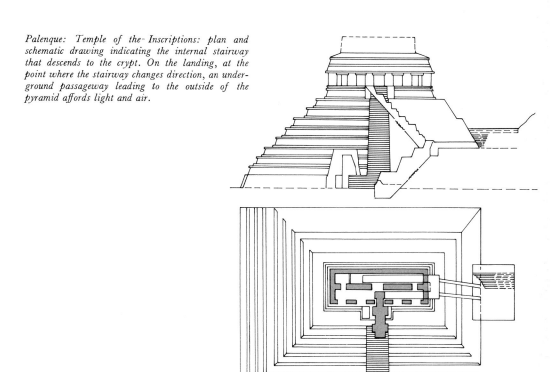

Below:
Palenque: The eastern courtyard of the Palace. The stone panel is part of a series of bas-reliefs of slaves that flank the access stairway of Edifice C.

to be looking at the cross that stands to his right, which is a very ornate emblem like the one in the Temple of the Cross — with the mythical bird Moan perched on top. Serpents' heads come from the horizontal arms of the cross, which hold up a two-headed serpent that spews forth two manikins.

This bas-relief is brimming with symbolic meaning most difficult to interpret. Here all the major symbols of the Mayan civilization can be found. The god of death below could be linked with the subterranean world and could be the god of fecund earth: an eternal ambiguity of Mayan beliefs. Above, a man comes forth like life being born. His face is like the god of maize; he could also be an incarnation of germination. Here are authority and power, with the ceremonial stick holding up the quadripartite universe represented by the cross — an image of the world but also an image of time and the rotation of power. Finally, on top, the bird Moan could symbolize death.

This grandiose composition is bordered by glyphs, among which there are the sun, the moon, Venus and six men's heads. Another fifty-two glyphs, sculpted on the lateral faces of the slab, carry various dates that correspond to our year 633. In addition to its symbolic meaning, this extraordinary stone slab also had a utilitarian function: it protected a sarcophagus. The secret room in the center of the pyramid was thus a burial crypt.

Only in November 1952 was it possible to lift and move the enormous slab. The skeleton of a human — over whom red cinnabar had been sprinkled — lay in the tomb. Surrounding the cranium were fragments of jade that were later reconstructed into a marvelous mask. Of particular interest was a long clay tube in the form of an immense serpent that stretched out of the sarcophagus and up the stairway to the vertical stone slab that once closed up the vaulted corridor: this was the last link between the illustrious dead man and the world of the living.

Who was the important person who was buried there? A king? A priest? A priest-king? This question is still unanswered. The sepulcher lies six feet below ground level under the pyramid of the Temple of the Inscriptions, and the colossal weight of the sarcophagus and of the stone slab show that the crypt was built before any other construction. The pyramid was thus erected later, above the tomb, perhaps as a kind of commemoration. It would seem that the Temple of the Inscriptions and the pyramid that supports it are a funerary monument; inevitably this has raised the question of whether other pyramids at other Mayan sites may have been erected in honor of dead leaders.

Palenque: Temple of the Inscriptions. The facade of the temple is seventy-six feet wide; the pyramid that supports it is fifty-two feet high and is composed of nine overlaid terraces. An inscription bearing 620 sculpted glyphs gives the edifice its name. An internal stairway leads to a magnificent crypt that protects a lavish tomb (A.D. 633) set under the base of the pyramid. This is the only known example in Mayan architecture of a tomb within a pyramid.

Bonampak

The site of Bonampak, which means "city of painted walls," is famous for its frescoes. Prior to the site's discovery in 1946, archaeologists had found fragments of Mayan painting in Palenque and Yaxchilán, but the uncovering of the complete, preserved murals of Bonampak represented a significant step forward for the study of Mayan art and culture.

The circumstances surrounding the preservation of the Bonampak paintings were unusual. In the middle 1940s an American conscientious objector, Carlos Frey, was living in exile in the forests of Chiapas in Mexico, so integrated with the Lacandón Indians that he had married one of them. Twice, over a period of two years, he noticed that the Lacandón men stained their long tunics with red dots, loaded themselves with copal incense, and disappeared for several days. Finally he learned the annual custom — a pilgrimage every year at the end of February to places whose identity was kept rigorously secret. Each group of men supposedly had a spot all its own, unknown by the women, that was reserved for the god of the forest, Kananka, where it was forbidden to enter with cutting objects or with a stranger.

Frey had no idea that certain parts of the forest were chosen for this ritual because of the monuments they contained, and while the Lacandóns were reluctant at first, they eventually decided to take him with them — since he had married one of their women. When Frey reached the sacred site with the Lacandóns, he saw that the copal offerings took place in a ruined temple. He explored the temple only slightly, but soon after the pilgrimage, when he left Chiapas, he spoke of the temple to many Americans, but no one showed interest.

A few months later an explorer named Giles Healy also discovered the temple hidden in Chiapas. Healy, who was gathering material for a documentary film on the Lacandón Indians, made a careful investigation of the interior of the temple; in doing so, he discovered splendid colored frescoes beneath a thin layer of limestone. Fortunately, a high rate of humidity in the region had preserved the frescoes. For over a thousand years a steady infiltration of water had covered the paintings with limestone deposits. If the temple had been situated in a known, accessible place, the frescoes would undoubtedly have been damaged, like numerous other pre-Columbian frescoes; the combination of humidity, isolation, and the holy respect of the Lacandóns had helped to save them.

THE CREATION OF THE WORLD

It is most necessary to believe this. These are the precious stones which our Lord, the Father, has abandoned. This was his first repast, this balché, with which we, the ruling men revere him here. Very rightly they worshipped as true gods these precious stones, when the true God was established, our Lord God, the Lord of heaven and earth, the true God. Nevertheless, the first gods were perishable gods. Their worship came to its inevitable end. They lost their efficacy by the benediction of the Lord of Heaven, after the redemption of the world was accomplished, after the resurrection of the true God, the true Dios, when he blessed heaven and earth. Then was your worship abolished, Maya men. Turn away your hearts from your old religion.

This is the history of the world in those times, because it has been written down, because the time has not yet ended for making these books, these many explanations, so that Maya men may be asked if they know how they were born here in this country, when the land was founded.

The Book of Chilam Balam of Chumayel
(p. 98)

The Temple

Bonampak is situated in the northern part of Chiapas near the Lacanja River, a tributary of the Usumacinta. On the only hill in the area, eight groups of structures, arranged on artificial mounds at different levels, represent the isolated heart of the site. In front of this complex lies a rectangular plaza (350 × 200 feet), at the center of which rises Stele 1, bearing the date 785.

The Temple of the Paintings is set on the first platform, or mound. It is twenty-three feet high, thirteen feet wide, and fifty-four feet long. Its facade, divided by a cornice, is perforated in the upper part by three niches in which there are remains of stucco statues. In the lower part of the facade, under the cornice, three low doors correspond to the niches above and give access to the three decorated rooms in the temple. The complex is deceptively simple, giving no indication of the unusual murals inside.

A total vision of the paintings is impossible in one glance, and as stated earlier, a layer of limestone obscures many of the pictures. Indeed, for visitors who have seen the rooms of Bonampak as they are

Bonampak: Temple of the Frescoes. Room 1, west wall: above, four dignitaries dressed in long cotton mantles; below, a procession of musicians. A horizontal strip of glyphs (eighth century) separates the two scenes.

reproduced in the museum in Mexico City, the originals on the site may prove disappointing.

Stylistically, the frescoes depict realistic scenes of social life in a manner that makes no attempt to create the illusion of movement. Nuance and perspective are omitted, and composition does not seem to have interested the Mayan artist. Background colors instead of landscapes suggest the setting for each mural: red for interior scenes, blue for the outdoors, and green spirals and red lines for vegetation. The faces of the figures are in profile, and action is expressed only through the attitude and position of the hands. More than a mere device or artifice, the style is reminiscent of a language of gestures to express facts or signify ideas.

The symbolic values of the mural colors predominate, while esthetic values assume a secondary role. The white of the tunics, the red and black of the bodies, and the green in the headdresses surely represent associations known and used by the people of that time. The quality of the draftsmanship, more than the colors, is what is outstanding artistically. The line is pure, and the artist knew how to depict the essence of this subject. The portraiture is good.

A close examination of these frescoes reveals that they were executed in three phases. First, persons and objects were drawn in light red lines on a layer of neutral-colored plaster from one to two inches thick. Second, the surfaces marked out by the lines were filled in with colors, vegetable or mineral: blue, red, green, black, yellow, and various color combinations obtained by mixing these basic colors. Finally, the original lines were touched up with a thin black line.

Ethnographic Scenes

In the first of the three rooms, on the left, a group of actors or priests appear to get ready to perform a ceremonial dance in which they will impersonate the gods of the earth. Two lines, of five and seven persons, converge on two other persons. Each of the figures wears a long, delicate white tunic decorated with shells (symbols of the earth). To the right of this group and above, the tallest personage sits cross-legged on a throne between two ladies-in-waiting. Behind, a servant holds a child in his arms. Dignified spectators witness the beginnings of the ceremony, and three gentlemen on the right appear to adorn themselves with jaguar hides, bracelets, necklaces, and jade pearls.

In the lower part of the fresco, the men are ready for the ceremony, crowned with water lilies. An orchestra with twelve musicians moves forward from the left, the first five shaking rattlers, followed by a drummer who beats on a huge drum and three other players who strike turtle shells with goat horns. Two parasol-bearers precede the dancers who appear to impersonate the gods. Two trumpet players and another musician bring up the rear of this procession.

Five of the actors representing the gods are concealed under frightful masks. They wear headdresses and earrings in the form of water lilies, which are emblems of the earth's generosity, and are the same as those worn by gods when they are in direct relation with the earth. The enormous, open jaws of the crocodile god are followed by the crab god with its aggressive claws. Then comes a person impersonating *Man* — the old god of the earth and of the number five, bearing a huge water lily that covers part of his face; under his arm he holds the glyph *tun*, his insignia. Then come the fourth and fifth divinities: the first with a pointed-face mask, and the other with the letter or sign "T" in his eyes, the symbol of germination, and with antennas in front of his mouth. The last participant in the group is not masked, but wears a large jade pearl necklace and a water lily wig or headdress; he appears to impersonate the god of maize. The abundance of detail in these scenes is surprising compared to other examples of Mayan art. For the first time,

Bonampak: Temple of the Frescoes. Room 1 west wall: the procession of musicians (as reconstructed at the National Museum of Anthropology, Mexico City).

Bonampak: Temple of the Frescoes. Room 1, south wall: portrait of five dignitaries (as reconstructed at the National Museum of Anthropology, Mexico City).

On the following pages:
Bonampak: Temple of the Frescoes. It is still impossible to decipher the meaning of this painting.

Bonampak: Temple of the Frescoes. Room 2.
Detail from a painting on the north wall,
depicting a prisoner (eighth century).

A HARSH KATUN PROPHESIED

Katun 5 Ahau is the fourth katun. The katun is established at Ichcaanzihoo. Harsh is its face, harsh its tidings, to the ruler. There is affliction of the offspring of woman and man, when it comes. Then begins the vexation by the devil in the world. Then came the blinding of the face of the god, the face of Kauil, in the four changing heavens, the four changing roads. Then hanging comes to the world. The red rattlesnake raises its head to bite; the holiloch raises its head to bite. Men and women have few children. Then came. . . the end of the cigar, after the lord of the world was created. . . he heard the dance. . . There is the red flowered thing, the red xulab, the red uayah-cab, the accessory of the rattle of the giver of our hearts in tribute through misery and vexation. It is the opossum chieftain, the fox chieftain, the *ah-pic* chieftain, the blood-sucking chieftain, the avaricious ones of the town. He is set up perchance, and then it is that your drum is beaten, my younger brother my elder brother. He who lies in wait for you on all fours is among you, the toliloch. It is his katun. The Plumeria flower is his chair, as he sits on his throne. He is publicly seen in the market-place on his mat, the two-day occupant of the throne, the two-day occupant of the mat. They deceive the town, the two town officials, the chieftain opossum and he who lies in wait on all fours. They bring the pestilence, they are the cause of. . . ; there was little of it formerly. You then called them the Itzá. The rattle of the katun is shaken; there is the treachery of the katun at Tancah Mayapán. There is the great tribute of Zuyua. The kinkajou claws the back of the jaguar amid the affliction of the katun, amid the affliction of the year; they are greedy for dominion. Many hangings are the charge of the katun, when the chiefs of the town are hung there. There is an end to the misery of the Maya men when suddenly the men of Uaymil come to take vengeance on the world.

The Book of Chilam Balam of Chumayel
(*pp. 152–53*)

realistic masks, musical instruments, and other objects are depicted, and the importance of religious ceremonies is emphasized.

The second room depicts a war-like scene. The first scene here presents an expedition of warriors wearing simple short tunics, head-dresses, and jewels. Armed with spears, they attack nude, defenseless farmers, and hold them prisoners with conventional gesture of holding them by the hair. The second scene shows the judgment of the prisoners. The captured men, terrorized, appear before the enemy leader. One of the prisoners is dead, and three others have bleeding fingers. (A head cut off its trunk lies on a bed of leaves.) A victorious warrior cuts a hole in the fourth victim's finger. The murals here seem to depict a surprise attack, or raid, carried out in order to get prisoners for sacrifices.

In the third room of murals, the dignitary of the first room is surrounded by his women. He has put on the long tunic, apparently reserved for the rites of sacrificing one's own blood, and is making a hole in his tongue. A servant offers him two cords of thorns, while another servant readies the large vase used to collect the blood on pieces of bark — bark that has been soaked with rubber and copal incense which will then be burnt in homage to the gods. (This was a custom in central Mexico when the Spanish arrived.) Some dignitaries watch these rites, as does a child, perhaps the son of the officiant, who is cuddled in the arms of a lady-in-waiting. Twelve men advance, bearing a litter on which a small figure with grotesque features lies. Finally, while the arms and legs of a sacrifice victim are being bound, the spectators watch the movements of ten lavishly dressed dancers who wear quetzal feathers in their hair.

Then the sky would fall, it would fall down upon the earth, when the four gods, the four Bacabs, were set up, who brought about the destruction of the world. Then, after the destruction of the world was completed, they placed a tree to set up in its order the yellow cock oriole. Then the white tree of abundance was set up. A pillar of the sky was set up, a sign of the destruction of the world; that was the white tree of abundance in the north. Then the black tree of abundance was set up in the west for the black-breasted picoy to sit upon. Then the yellow tree of abundance was set up in the south, as a symbol of the destruction of the world, for the yellow-breasted picoy to sit upon, for the yellow cock oriole to sit upon, the yellow timid mut. Then the green tree of abundance was set up in the center of the world as a record of the destruction of the world.

The plate of another katun was set up and fixed in its place by the messengers of their lord. The red Piltec was set at the east of the world to conduct people to his lord. The white Piltec was set at the north of the world to conduct people to his lord. Lahun Chaan was set at the west to bring things to his lord. The yellow Piltec was set at the south to bring things to his lord. But it was over the whole world that Ah Uuc Cheknal was set up. He came from the seventh stratum of the earth, when he came to fecundate Itzam-kab-ain, when he came with the vitality of the angle between earth and heaven. They moved among the four lights, among the four layers of the stars. The world was not lighted; there was neither day nor night nor moon. Then they perceived that the world was being created. Then creation dawned upon the world.

The Book of Chilam Balam of Chumayel
(pp. 99–101

The Bonampak frescoes depict Mayan activities and scenes of life that are not represented elsewhere. Here, innumerable details are revealed about the customs, weapons, musical instruments, dances, family groups, battles and sacrifices of the Mayan people. It has been established that religious ceremonies were most important for the Maya, and here their social character is confirmed.

At the same time, some of the scenes raise questions about our ideas of Mayan life. Thus, the presence of women in these ceremonies might contradict the theory that the Mayas had an exclusively male social structure. Also, the warriors brandishing spears, defeating their enemies and sacrificing prisoners, somewhat alters the early image of the Maya as a peaceful people. Two of the three panels under the entrance to the Temple of the Paintings present a warrior chief in the act of knocking down an adversary, while at the same time getting ready to thrust his heavy spear into his body. This type of activity was not found in Mayan sculpture before these paintings. Thus in A.D. 800, the date of the paintings, the men of Bonampak appear more revengeful than their brothers in Yaxchilán, on the other bank of the Usumacinta. The reason why these changes in attitude appear to have taken place remains unanswered.

On the following page:
Bonampak: Temple of the Frescoes. Room 1, north wall: a group of masked dancers from the lower fresco (as reconstructed at the National Museum of Anthropology, Mexico City).

THE POST-CLASSIC PERIOD

The Mayan Texts

In addition to the many Mayan inscriptions at archaeological sites, we have been fortunate in finding a fair number of Mayan books that confirm, amplify, and explain much about the remains in stone, add still a further dimension, and raise many more questions. Many newcomers to the Mayan world may at first be confused by the fact that the Mayan language is said to be as yet undeciphered, while so much seems to be known about — and from — their written texts. This apparent contradiction is resolved once it is realized that scholars can read most of the writing concerned with dates, gods, astronomical observations, and a few other matters — the very subjects of so much of the extant writings and inscriptions. A certain amount can also be inferred — by context, by comparison with other texts, and by scholarly "detective work." And there is no denying that the starting point for modern knowledge of the Mayan writings has been the work of the Spanish priest, Diego de Landa; elsewhere in this book, we described at some length the irony of his career: the man who helped to erase so much of the Mayan heritage and yet who ended by preserving so much of what we now know.

But although Landa and his fellow Spaniards destroyed all too many of the original Mayan texts, several did survive; three of these (along with many others from other Mexican Indians) have ended up in Europe, where they were brought by priests and soldiers during the early decades of the Spanish Conquest. (An American scholar announced in 1971 that he had found what he claims to be part of a fourth such Mayan book, but there has not been time to evaluate its true worth.) These original Mayan books are known as codices (the plural form of codex, a book in manuscript); they were made by peeling long strips of bark (from a fig tree), which was then beaten and soaked in resin; dried, it was covered with a thin sizing of lime. On this surface, the Mayan priest-scribes — like the monks of medieval Europe — wrote and painted the glyphs or script, the numbers, the images of gods and animals in various colors: black, yellow, green, blue, and red. The strips were about eight inches high and ran to several yards in length; they were folded, screenlike, with each fold becoming a "page" of about six inches in width; both sides were written on, first on all the front sides, and then around and onto the back sides of the pages.

The three important Mayan codices are generally known today by the names of the cities where they are now preserved in libraries. Although all were written down long after the classic phase of Mayan culture, they contain traditional materials dating from centuries earlier, materials that were handed down by word-of-mouth or by older written texts. The glyphs in the codices are identical to certain glyphs sculpted on monuments at various Mayan sites as well as to those in Landa's book, thus establishing the continuity of the Mayan culture across many centuries and throughout many hundreds of square miles.

The most valuable of the three is the Dresden Codex, which has belonged to the library in Dresden (now in East Germany) since 1739. It is almost four yards long and contains seventy-eight pages; essentially it is a treatise on astronomy (including accurate tables for predicting eclipses), but it also contains numerous horoscopes and some indications of ritual practices. It has been of crucial help to scholars in understanding the Mayan calendar and chronology. It is not only the most beautiful of the three, but also the oldest, dating from about the eleventh century.

The Madrid Codex (where it is in the National Library) is the longest of the three, with its 112 pages running to almost eight yards. Probably it is not much older than the fifteenth century. It is mainly a book about divination and ceremonies, like a memorandum to be used by the priest-diviners. The Paris Codex (located in the National Library) is no older than the Madrid Codex. In poor and incomplete condition, it is less than five feet long, with twenty-two pages; it deals

Madrid Codex: Page 30. Upper part: God B (Chac, the rain god) stands on the serpent's head; to the right, on the serpent's tail, the goddess I (Ixchel, wife of Itzamná). Both gods pour water from containers. Lower part: the goddess Ixchel has a serpent on her head. Jets of water pour from her body. Two animals on her outstretched hands spew water; two animals crouch on her right foot; on her left is God B. The whole illustration symbolizes the rain season.

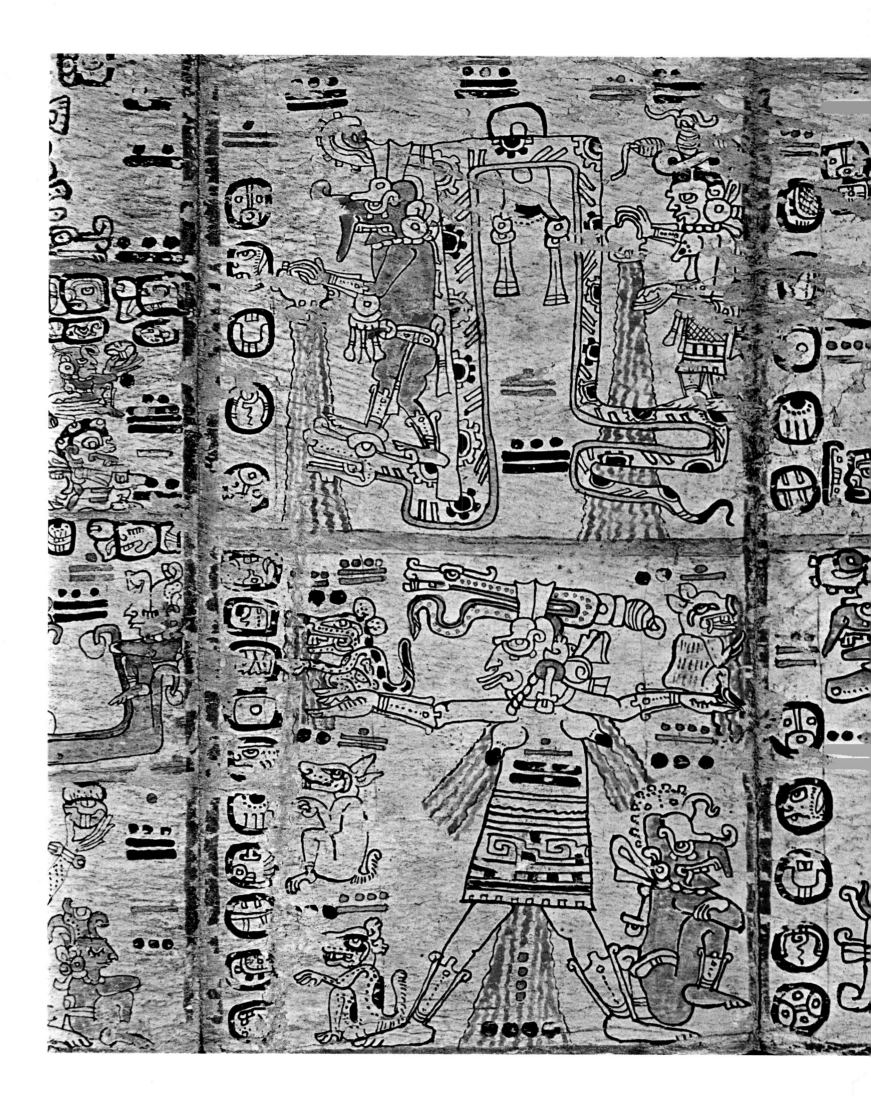

with divination and with ceremonies and prophecies involved with the cycle of time.

In addition to these still largely unread Mayan texts, several books were written down after the Spanish Conquest by natives who transcribed their Mayan language into our familiar European script. The three most important of these books have provided the excerpts for the "anthology" that runs throughout the margins of this volume, and we should know a bit about each.

Popol Vuh was first written down in the mid-sixteenth century by some anonymous, but educated, member of the Quiché Maya Indians; although he wrote in a somewhat elaborate literary style, he obviously drew upon the age-old traditions of his people and the result is a true "national epic." The original version was lost, but not before it had been copied at the end of the seventeenth century by a Dominican priest. Brasseur de Bourbourg carried this copy off to France in the late nineteenth century, but it has since ended up in the Newberry Library in Chicago. *Popol Vuh* is a sacred book that provides considerable information about the cosmogony, mythology, religion, traditions, and history of the Quiché Maya (whose descendants still live on the plateaus of Guatemala).

The Annals of the Cakchiquels was first written down at the end of the sixteenth century by several Indians of the Cakchiquels, a Mayan people who lived in the mountainous regions of Guatemala; they were closely related to the Quiché Maya, and this book coincides with many of the details in the *Popol Vuh*. The existent copy of *The Annals* was made in the mid-seventeenth century, and contains certain additions that bring it up to the year 1604. Because the book was kept for some time in the town of Sololá, it is sometimes known as *Memorial de Sololá;* it was also called the *Memorial de Tecpan-Atitlan* (after the region and lake where the Cakchiquels lived) by Brasseur de Bourbourg, who took the original to France and made a French translation. When his possessions were sold in Paris in 1885, an American scholar, Daniel Brinton, bought the manuscript and presented it to the library of the museum of the University of Pennsylvania, in Philadelphia. *The Annals* is a more straightforward history than *Popol Vuh*, and recounts the story of the Cakchiquels up to their conquest by the Spaniards; it also contains much mythological, legendary, and popular material that had been handed down orally for many generations.

The Chilam Balam of Chumayel, unlike the other two major source books of Maya culture, is attributed to a historical individual, the last great prophet of the Maya. "Chilam" was a title, something close to "interpreter of the gods;" "Balam" was his family name (although it also meant "jaguar"). Chilam Balam seems to have been a real man who lived in the last decades of the fifteenth century and into the early years of the sixteenth. He prophesied that strangers from the east would come to the Maya lands and set up a new religion; since the Spaniards came so quickly after Chilam Balam foretold this, he seems to have gained a reputation as a great prophet. Ten or eleven versions of the book attributed to him have survived, and the best of these is the one that belonged to the Chumayel, a Maya people in the northern Yucatán. The Chumayel version known today dates only from 1782 (and even this manuscript has since been lost) but it draws upon much older materials, including hieroglyphic writings. In addition to the prophecies of Chilam Balam himself, it contains various historical sections, creation myths, rituals, the native catechism, an almanac, and medical subjects. Primitive though this and the other books and codices may be, they remain the tangible links between the ancient Maya world and our curiosity about it.

Chichén-Itzá: The Castillo, or Temple of Kukulkán, seen from the Temple of the Warriors. In the left foreground, a standard-bearer. The structures date from the beginning of the eleventh century A.D.

Chichén-Itzá: General plan
1. Cenote (Well) of Sacrifices
2. Ball Court
3. Wall of Skulls
4. Temple of the Eagles
5. Tomb of Chacmool, or Platform of Venus
6. Temple of the Warriors
7. Temple of Kukulkán, or Castillo
8. The Thousand Columns
9. Market place
10. Tomb of the High Priest
11. Cenote of Xtoloc (civil well)
12. Colored House
13. The Caracol (Snail)
14. House of Painted Reliefs
15. Palace of the Nuns
16. La Iglesia
17. Akab K'Zib ("Obscure Writing")
18. Road to Mérida

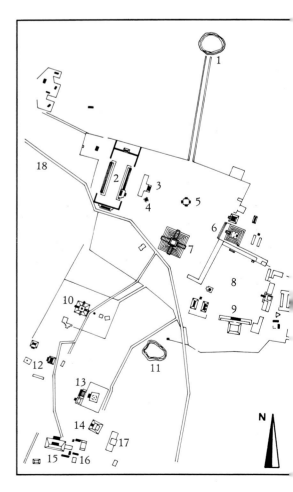

Chichén-Itzá

Chichén-Itzá was an important and well-known holy center that was once one of the great pilgrimage sites in the Yucatán. The etymology of Chichén-Itzá, "mouth of the well of the Itzá," emphasizes its significance. In this flat, arid peninsula of 93,000 square miles, a series of natural wells, *cenotes*, penetrate the limestone to a vast underground water-bearing stratum. Without this water, life would not be possible in the Yucatán. Chichén-Itzá has two large cenotes, and several of its important monuments are situated between them.

Regarding the ethnic origins of the peoples known as the Itzá, opinions are divided and scholars disagree. Bishop de Landa and the *Books of Chilam Balam* narrate that from the fifth century on, a wave of emigrants, the Itzá, came from the Mayan lands of Petén and went to the Yucatán. After a stay in the north, they then settled in Tabasco (a Mexican state neighboring the Yucatán). Later, the same chronicles tell of the Itzá going to the Yucatán in the tenth century — arriving from the southeast (apparently from Tabasco). Possibly these were the descendants of the Itzá who had emigrated from Petén originally. Some authorities say that the Itzá were first a group of Mexicanized Chontol-Maya living in Tabasco, later settling in Champoton on the coast of Campeche, and then moving up the coast. In fact, no one can describe the origins of the Itzá with any certainty, but there is evidence that they set up a capital in Chichén-Itzá during the *katun* 4 Ahau (A.D. 967–987), where they soon became the subjects of a Toltec invader, "Kukulkán." The name Kukulkán is in effect the simple Mayan translation of "Quetzalcoatl," the Plumed Serpent (*kukul:* precious feathers; *can:* serpent), who was the most popular divinity in central Mexico for hundreds of years and whose exploits assume a legendary tone.

THE DISCOVERY OF CHICHÉN-ITZÁ

Ahau was the katun when they sought and discovered Chichén-Itzá. There it was that miraculous things were performed for them by their lords. Four divisions they were, when the four divisions of the nation, as they were called, went forth. From Kincolahpeten in the east one division went forth. From Nacocob in the north one division came forth. But one division came forth from Holtun Zuyua in the west. One division came forth from Four-peaked Mountain, Nine Mountains is the name of the land.

The Book of Chilam Balam of Chumayel
(*p. 139*)

Chichén-Itzá: The Castillo. The gigantic support for the temple is a pyramid seventy-eight feet high that raises its nine steps on a 179-foot square foundation. The terraces (or steps) symbolize the nine underground worlds. The temple proper on the top, is a simple construction nineteen feet long and fourteen feet wide.

Chichén-Itzá: Castillo. Schematic drawing and plan.

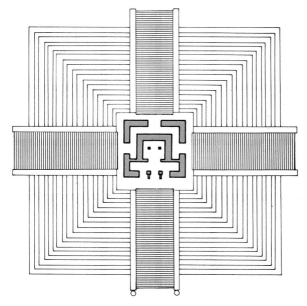

Left, above:
Chichén-Itzá: The head of the Chacmool (a typical Toltec stone sculpture piece) from inside the Castillo. Inside the pyramid, a tunnel leads to the small subterranean temple of the original, primitive pyramid, where there is found this unusual statue of Chacmool with ivory eyes, nose and teeth.

Left, below:
Chichén-Itzá: The Red Jaguar of the Castillo. In the second chamber of the inner temple of the Castillo this statue of a life-size stone jaguar opens its jaws exposing flint fangs. Its skin is rendered speckled by eighty tiny pieces of jade; the two balls for its eyes are also jade. A solar disk is attached to the animal's back.

FOREIGNERS COME TO THE YUCATÁN

Today I have written down that in the year 1541 the foreigners first arrived from the east at Ecab, as it was called. In that year occurred their arrival at the port of Ecab, at the village of Nacom Balam, on the first day of the year in which Katun 11 Ahau fell. After the Itzá were dispersed, it was fifteen score years when the foreigners arrived. It was after the town of Zaclahtun was depopulated, after the town of Kinchil Coba was depopulated, after the town of Chichén-Itzá was depopulated, after the town on the Uxmal side of the range of hills, the great town of Uxmal as it is called, was depopulated, as well as Kabah. It was after the towns of Zeye, Pakam, Homtun, at the town of Tix-calom-kin, and Ake, Holtun Ake, were depopulated.

It was after the town of Emal Chac was depopulated, Izamal, where the daughter of the true God, Lord of Heaven, descended, the Queen, the Virgin, the miraculous one. When the ruler said: "The shield of Kinich Kakmo shall descend," he was not declared ruler here. It was she, the miraculous one, the merciful one, who was so declared here. "The rope shall descend, the cord shall descend from heaven. The word shall descend from heaven." There was rejoicing over his reign by the other towns when they said this, but he was not declared their ruler at Emal.

Then the great Itzá went away. Thirteen four-hundreds were the four-hundreds of their thousands, and fifteen four-hundreds, the four-hundreds of their hundreds, the leading men among them, the heathen Itzá. But many supporters went with them to feed them. Thirteen measures of corn per head were their quota, and nine measures and three handsful of grain. From many small towns the magicians went with them also.

The Book of Chilam Balam of Chumayel
(pp. 81–83)

On the following pages:
Chichén-Itzá: Temple of the Warriors and The Thousand Columns (dating from the beginning of the eleventh century).

On page 98
Chichén-Itzá: Temple of the Warriors. In the foreground is a Chacmool, behind which a series of columns forms a serpent. This is similar to Toltec works.

The Plumed Serpent Legends

When the Spanish arrived in Mexico in the sixteenth century, "Quetzalcoatl" represented the god of wind for the Aztecs. He also symbolized water and fertility, and by extension, rain and vegetation. Centuries earlier, in Teotihuacan, the great theocratic city on the plateau of central Mexico which flourished well before the Toltec and Aztec invasions, Quetzalcoatl occupied the most important place in the pantheon.

At the end of the eighth century, when the Toltec tribes (who spoke the *Nahua* tongue, and were specialists in human sacrifice) infiltrated the territory of Teotihuacan and destroyed the city, they apparently adopted the image of the Plumed Serpent and gave it a *Nahuan* name — Quetzalcoatl. The legend of the Plumed Serpent then spread all over Mexico in the wake of the conquerors. With an essential and beneficent power as the "carrier of rain," Quetzalcoatl soon became the most important Toltec god — so much so that his name alone assumed magical overtones and became the supreme title reserved for king-priests. In the thirteenth century, when the Aztec warriors (who also spoke *Nahuan*) began to take over the Mexican central plateau, they assimilated the traditions, legends, and historical exploits of the Toltecs. Their accounts say that the fifth Toltec sovereign ("Quetzalcoatl") lived fifty-two years, from 947 to 999. This king-priest had been called Ce-acatl (one-cane), which derived from the name of the year of his birth, until he was elected ruler over Tollan.

This Quetzalcoatl was apparently a very ugly man, who wore a beard. But he was said to be pious, just, benevolent, a great leader, and with him the golden age of the Toltecs began. The golden age was short, however, because this king tried to abolish human sacrifices and thereby made many enemies. His idea was to substitute the sacrifices with offerings of flowers, incense, butterflies, and maize bread. His notions displeased the military chiefs, who then tried to make him fall into disgrace. All their attempts failed, the chronicles say, until the day when they gave him a mirror. Frightened by his own ugliness and the deep wrinkles in his face, he agreed to drink a highly alcoholic beverage in order to get rid of his unpleasant appearance. He sang, drank again, forgot his dignity, and fell into great dissoluteness. The next day he left Tollan in shame and took the road to Tlapallan to the east.

Quetzalcoatl died in the year one-cane, the same name of the year of his birth, having lived (according to the Toltec beliefs) a complete cycle of time. (When his heart reached Venus, they believed, the planet then took on the name Ce-acatl.) The Aztec chronicles emphasize that the bearded king of Tollan in the west (land of the color white) went to the east (land of the colors red and black) with the aim of reaching the sea and dying amidst flames. These pre-Columbian accounts add that Quetzalcoatl had declared, before departing, that he would return from the east by sea and restore his Toltec kingdom.

When Cortés arrived in Aztec territory, the emperor Montezuma thought that the ancient Indian prophecy had become a reality. The details seemed to fit in perfectly: the foreigner wore a beard, was white (the symbolic color of the west and hence of Quetzalcoatl), and he arrived from the east by sea — in the year one-cane! Thus, instead of crushing the Spaniard and his men with the hundreds of thousands of warriors at his disposal, Montezuma hastened to make offerings to the gods and to proffer gifts to Cortés. Among these gifts was the lavish headdress of quetzal feathers, which according to tradition had belonged to Quetzalcoatl himself. In this way Montezuma virtually handed over his empire to the Spaniards.

This semi-legendary account of the Plumed Serpent is closely connected to Chichén-Itzá and tends to confirm the evidence set out in Bishop de Landa's book and in the *Books of Chilan Balam*. According to the Mayan sources, the Toltec leader "Kukulkán" arrived in Chichén-Itzá between 967 and 987. According to Aztec sources, "Quetzalcoatl" ascended the throne of Tollan in 977 and then abandoned the

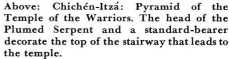

Below: Chichén-Itzá: Temple of the Warriors. The stone altar. The two caryatids that support the heavy altar reveal the Toltec origin of this monument.

Above: Chichén-Itzá: Pyramid of the Temple of the Warriors. The head of the Plumed Serpent and a standard-bearer decorate the top of the stairway that leads to the temple.

land, went east, and died in 999. The data from the two different sources appear to agree chronologically, but the mixture of fact and fiction is confusing, and whether these two personages were, in fact, the same is not certain.

In the Aztec chronicles, the city of Tollan (where Quetzalcoatl first reigned) always appears to be legendary. But in 1863, the French traveler Désiré Charnay claimed that the mythical Tollan did indeed exist — near the village of Tula northeast of Mexico City. Historians and public opinion attached little importance to his assertions, however, when he stated that Chichén-Itzá was a grandiose copy of the city of Tollan (or Tula), and was thereby a creation of the Toltecs.

The relationship Charnay established between these two sites has since been borne out by investigation. The excavations of Chichén-Itzá began in 1925 under the auspices of the Carnegie Institution of Washington and the Mexican Department of Anthropology. They were directed by Sylvanus G. Morley and lasted seventeen years. Tula was later excavated under the direction of W. Jimenez-Moreno, who after the discovery of an ancient map furnished proof that Tollan, the Toltec capital, was not Teotihuacan (as people thought in 1939), but was Tula. This site, in the state of Hidalgo, was then established as having been founded and inhabited by the Toltecs. In 1940, seventy-five years after Charnay's affirmations, the first excavations at Tula confirmed its close ties with Chichén-Itzá and it was then hypothesized that the two cities were constructed under the supervision of the same leader — possibly Quetzalcoatl — who became known as Kukulkán when he settled in the Yucatán.

The Temple of Kukulkán

Many of the edifices at Chichén-Itzá, then, are more Toltec than Mayan. The only group that can be considered pure Mayan is in the "old" section of the center (Chichén Viejo), which will be discussed last. For the most part, the Toltec influence is very significant in the post-classical Mayan structures on this site.

The most important construction in Chichén-Itzá is the Temple of Kukulkán. This temple was called Pyramida del Castillo by the Spaniards because the conquistador Francisco de Montejo set up his headquarters there after the conquest of the Yucatán. The gigantic support of the temple is a terraced pyramid seventy-eight feet high resting on a 179-foot square base. At the center of each of the four sides of the pyramid a ninety-one step stairway (enclosed by stone ramps that rest on serpents' heads) leads up to the temple, which dominates the entire site. This monumental pyramid is interesting in that its nine terraces symbolize the nine regions of the underworld (as conceived by the Mayans), and the number of the steps of the four stairways — plus the one extra entrance step to the temple — correspond to the 365 days of the civil year.

The temple on the top of the pyramid, a bit overwhelmed by the imposing volume of its support, is a simple construction (14 × 19 feet) with two central pillars around which runs a six-foot-wide gallery, or corridor. The thick northern, southern, and western facades contain simple openings; on the northern side, the temple opens on to a portico with three columns, typically Toltec, which represent the Plumed Serpent.

Inside the pyramid, a stairway leads to another construction buried under the "Castillo" complex: the nucleus of the pyramid. The dis-

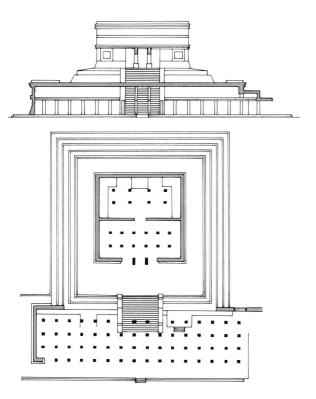

Chichén-Itzá: Temple of the Warriors. Schematic drawing and plan, including the courtyard of the columns.

Chichén-Itzá: Temple of the Warriors. The bas-reliefs on the columns depict Toltec warriors. The sacred ball court is in the background.

covery of one edifice inside another is not exceptional, for the Maya of the classical period often demolished their temples in order to build new ones in the same place. The Aztecs also, like the Toltecs, followed this procedure in obedience to a ritual "edict" that required the destruction of all temples at the beginning of every fifty-two year cycle. As a sign of new life, new sanctuaries sprang up on the enlarged pyramids. At Chichén-Itzá, however, the ancient temple remained intact, along with its "furnishings," inside the later edifice. It was thus revealed that the earlier double-vaulted hall and the frieze between the cornices of the facade were of Mayan style. In the first hall archaeologists discovered a Chacmool, an essentially Toltec stone sculpture piece representing a life-size man lying on his back, the upper part of his body raised on his elbows, his knees bent, and his head turned away, with a round, plate-like hat on his head. His fingernails and toenails, and his teeth and eyes (with a black mark in the center) were of polished bone. In the second hall they found an essentially Mayan sculpture — a stone tiger painted red, its body encrusted with mother-of-pearl, in the form of a throne — similar to the ones already noted in classical Mayan cities.

Chichén-Itzá: The Thousand Columns. Rows of pillars around the Temple of the Warriors are composed of overlaid cylindrical sections with square plinths on top.

Sixty grandiose quadrangular pillars surround another edifice at Chichén-Itzá, the Temple of the Warriors. East of the "Castillo," this temple flanks the great plaza around which Toltec structures lie. These stone colonnades originally constituted the sub-structure of this temple and held up the heavy beamed roofs that long ago collapsed.

Every side of these pillars is covered with bas-reliefs that reveal traces of painting. They represent disciplined warriors standing at attention, ready for combat. Bands decorated with turquoise or eagle feathers bind their foreheads, and their accessories — sandals, earrings, nose ornaments, leather belts, breast plates of gold or precious stones chiseled in the shape of a butterfly — are all reminders of their Toltec origin. The left arm of each warrior is bound in a thick leather band, a sort of shield to ward off blows, while each right hand holds a javelin or an *atlatl*, a short, flat wooden spear-throwing device with a large groove in the center in which the spear or dart was placed before being hurled. In comparison with these warriors, the scenes at the earlier site, Bonampak, appear relatively peaceful. In reality these columns are

Chichén-Itzá: One column of the Temple of the Warriors. This bas-relief depicts a Toltec warrior with a serpent headdress and a typical Toltec ornament through his nose. Precious quetzal feathers cover his body.

not so much proof of a new architectural influence as they are a reminder of a new "order" forced on the people of the Yucatán at the end of the tenth century: the Order of Toltec warriors.

Inside the rows of columns, a pyramid (130 × 130 feet) with four terraces rises to a height of thirty-seven feet. Two statues of standard bearers guard the top of the stairs leading to the last terrace, where a Chacmool image keeps watch over the temple entrance. Two pillars, elongated into the shape of a plumed serpent, frame this entrance, and twenty pillars stand that once supported the ceiling of the two halls in the temple. A detachment of eighty warriors on the sides of the halls give a detailed picture of weapons and ornaments, and four caryatids hold up the large stone altar at the end of the temple. Similarities between the edifices and interiors at Chichén-Itzá and Tula are evident, although the Toltec creations at Chichén-Itzá seem more complete, fully realized, and better styled than the ones in Tula.

During the excavations on the nucleus of this pyramid, archaeologists discovered the vestiges of still another structure which seems to be a small model of the Temple of the Warriors. The sides of this pyramid measure seventy-eight feet, and the base of its temple measures sixty feet. This structure also has a series of pillars, which are obviously less imposing than the ones surrounding the larger temple.

Painted in violent colors, these pillars covered the walls of the temple. On a red background, bright yellow bodies of men and green ornaments bear witness to a very uncertain art, still groping for realization. Despite efforts made with the most modern techniques, however, it has been impossible to conserve these frescoes; the potassium nitrate that forms upon contact with the air literally turns them to dust. A hypostyle hall (49 × 156 feet) with a roof held up by sixty-two pillars in the shape of sculptured warriors, precedes the first edifice. An investigation of the rubble has led to the discovery of a Chacmool that probably towered over the temple entrance. A frog motif decorates its headdress.

Edifices Bordering the Plaza

Three small edifices border the "Castillo" plaza, which once was the heart of Chichén-Itzá. They are not striking, architecturally speaking, but each of them reveals a particular characteristic of the foreign culture that penetrated the Yucatán in the wake of the Toltec invasion.

The Tomb of Chacmool is a square platform (81 × 81 feet), with one long step on each side. Augustus Le Plongeon, an American adventurer of French origin, gifted with a great imagination, discovered here in 1875 one of the "Chacmool" statues typical of the Toltec civilization; hence the name of the edifice. Plongeon was the first to refer to these sculptures as Chacmool, and even today scholars wonder what induced him to use this name which means "red jaguar" and bears no relation to the sculpture itself. However, the name has become widespread and is now used by everyone to designate this type of Toltec figure. All of these stone statues are alike, with the two hands holding a stone plate on the abdomen. In general they are found at temple entranceways, and some scholars claim that they were set there in order to receive the offerings of the faithful. This would appear too Christian and Western a theory, as access to the temples in this culture was strictly reserved for priests, initiates, and the sacrifice victims. In later centuries the Aztecs represented the rain god Tlaloc in the "Chacmool" form holding a stone plate (the *cuautxicalli*) on his belly in order to receive the heart and blood of human victims. It may be that the original Toltec Chacmool had a similar function.

Certain objects depicted in the bas-reliefs of the Tomb of Chacmool

Chichén-Itzá: A Chacmool. This stone sculpture, strictly Toltec, was the first of its kind to be discovered at Chichén-Itzá. It was found in 1875 by Augustus Le Plongeon, who improperly christened it "Chacmool" (red jaguar). The name has been maintained, however, and is still commonly used. (National Museum of Anthropology, Mexico City)

are of interest. There are two motifs: Venus in the form of a half-serpent, half-bird, symbol of Quetzalcoatl; and the hieroglyph for Venus coupled with the sign for the fifty-two-year cycle. These symbols indicate the extent to which the Toltecs venerated the morning star; there is a growing tendency to designate this edifice with the name "Platform of Venus."

The Temple of the Eagles, a small terrace similar to the preceding one, is decorated with a bas-relief frieze of eagles and jaguars. For the Toltecs these animals were warrior symbols; here their claws and talons clutch human hearts — a significant allegory for the men from the north who worshiped blood-thirsty gods and had nothing in common, culturally speaking, with the Maya. The Toltecs were not interested in conquering time by means of complicated calendars;

Chichén-Itzá: Panorama of the Sacred Ball Court flanked by the Temple of the Jaguars. The playing field measures 309 x 114 feet and is the most significant in all Mayan territory.

Chichén-Itzá: Temple of the Jaguars. At the entrance a stone jaguar serves as an altar. One side of the temple overlooks the large plaza of the Castillo, opposite the Temple of the Warriors; the upper part of the temple opens onto the courtyard of the ball court.

rather, they sought to satisfy their cruel gods so that life would follow its normal course — or so that the stars would follow their course in the sky. The sun, they apparently believed, became worn out by his nightly journey, and needed fresh energy every morning, which only human blood could provide.

The Nahuan term *Tzompantli* (wall of skulls) designates the third structure bordering the plaza — a large rectangular platform (180 × 49 feet) which was used, as the bas-reliefs indicate, to support a type of fence on which the heads of sacrifice victims were impaled.

During the ceremony, a victim was placed on his back on a small stone cone by four assistants (*chaces*) whose job it was to keep the victim's arms and feet pulled back firmly on the ground. The victim thus arched his chest, into which the high priest made a long incision

with a flint knife under the victim's ribs. The priest then thrust both hands in and tore out the still-palpitating heart and placed it in the stone plates of Chacmool as an offering to the gods.

Decapitation of the victim followed, and the head was brought to the *Tzompantli* where it was impaled on a peg or stick of the fence. Some bas-reliefs indicate that eagles and jaguars had the responsibility of transporting the detached heads. The body was then cut into pieces and thrown from the top of the pyramid to the crowds below, who apparently seized the remains to use them for ritual banquets.

It is surprising to find this type of construction in a city supposedly built by Quetzalcoatl, who had lost the throne of Tula apparently because he wanted to abolish human sacrifices. But the chronicles tell us that the Plumed Serpent abandoned Chichén-Itzá after its foundation.

The Sacred Ball Game

The sacred ball game, which was widespread all over pre-Columbian America, was developed particularly in Central America. Every

Chichén-Itzá: The Sacred Ball Court and the east terrace, bordered by a long stone serpent. At the center of the field, one of the two stone rings through which the rubber ball must pass is set into the wall at a height of twenty-six feet.

Chichén-Itzá: Reconstruction of the sacred ball court
1. *Northern temple*
2. *Southern temple*
3. *Spectators' stand*
4. *Point in the wall where the stone rings are placed*
5. *Temple of the Jaguars*

On pages 110-111:
Chichén-Itzá: Bas-relief of the east terrace of the ball field. The captain of the winning team holds the head of the losing team's captain in his left hand. Seven serpents rise from the decapitated man's neck. In the center, the ball is decorated with a human skull; its half-closed jaws hold the symbol of death.

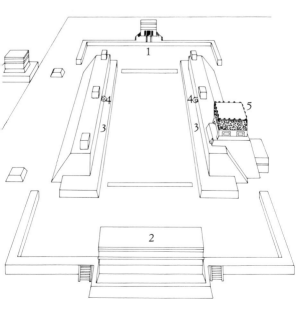

classical Mayan city had at least one playing field. The field at Chichén-Itzá is the most impressive in all Mexico and the three edifices built on its perimeter emphasize its importance: two little temples (or grandstands) at the two ends of the field, and the Temple of the Jaguars dominating the eastern wall. On one side this temple opens directly onto the great plaza of the Castillo, opposite the Temple of the Warriors, while the first floor of the temple overlooks the playing field from an elegant portico with serpentine columns. All the bas-reliefs on the columns, the stairways, and the walls, are in homage to Quetzalcoatl and to the Toltec warriors.

The playing field proper is 309 feet long and 114 feet wide. Two walls twenty-six feet high flank its entire length. At the center of the field two large stone rings are positioned near the top of each wall. Two long terraces for spectators run along the foot of the walls.

There were two teams in the game the Maya played. The idea was to make the rubber ball pass through the stone rings. It was against the rules to hit the ball with hands or feet; the players had to butt it with their shoulders, knees, hips or elbows. Further, the ball was not supposed to touch the ground. It must have been rare to see the ball pass through the ring, and the winning team was usually the one

committing the fewest errors: the ball touching the ground, hit out of bounds, or hit with the hand, etc. Spanish chroniclers, who had the fortune to witness numerous games, have provided these details on the game. The Aztecs were also fanatic about this game and every Aztec palace had its playing field. The games were played fiercely and the stakes were high; at times the entire population became involved. The chronicles reveal that Montezuma, the last Aztec emperor, had to go onto the field one day to break up a heated argument.

This ball game was apparently not a game demonstrating skill or sporting qualities, but rather a kind of "liturgical function" through which the gods manifested their desires. This explains the religious ceremony that surrounded everything concerning the ball game. On the eve of each match, the two teams prayed. The players asked the gods to render the ball favorable to them and to put charms and spells on their playing equipment — gloves, kneepads, shoulderpads, etc. The stone rings were also the object of numerous prayers, along with the ball, made of "magical" rubber. (Rubber was a first-rate incense, a

Chichén-Itzá: Wall of Skulls (Tzompantli). This terrace (some 200 feet long and 50 feet wide) extends along the open plaza opposite the Castillo. It is decorated with bas-reliefs depicting human skulls; the platform once supported a fence on which were impaled the heads of humans sacrificed to the gods.

precious offering, and possibly after the match the winning team offered the ball to the gods by burning it.) A drawing in the *Nuttall Codex* shows an altar of the Mixtec civilization on which a rubber ball is burning; the *Vienna Codex* shows a game being played in the sky as a flaming rubber ball swoops down.

It is difficult to believe that the losing team lost its life, but the bas-reliefs on the eastern terrace at Chichén-Itzá, bordered by a long stone serpent, are precise. The seven players of each team converge around a ball decorated with a human skull. Two large spirals rise out of the jaws of the skull, which are reminiscent of a serpent's forked tongue and also of the sign *miquiztli* which means "death" and which was the calendar day of the sun feasts and of Tezcatlipoca, the Toltec god of war. All the players in the scene are richly dressed in plumed helmets, large, thick girdles, and kneepads on the right leg. On their waists they wear a wooden object that looks like a mallet and has either a serpent's head or a monkey's head, or perhaps a small human skull, on its top. A serpent-shaped object that the players hold in their hands has not been identified.

In the central scene the first player on the team (on the left) holds in his right hand a flint knife of the type used for human sacrifices; in his left hand he holds the head of the first player of the opposing team, the losing team. The torso of the decapitated man is on its knees, and from his bleeding neck seven serpents writhe — the central snake in the shape of a luxuriant plant, full of flowers and fruit. (Seven players, seven serpents.) The number seven also symbolizes maize, and has a privileged place in the center of the fundamental numerical series in the magical Mayan calendar, from one to thirteen (described in detail in a later chapter). It could be that this central serpent represents the heart of man and the heart of an ear of corn, indicating a relationship in the ball game between the fertility rites and the decapitation rites. In the Nahuan codices the ball is identified with the sun; also the twisted serpents sculpted on the stone rings in the playing field probably symbolize the sky.

The sacred ball game could have been, then, a representation of the course of the sun, represented by the ball, with the result of the match determining the fertility of the earth. Or, perhaps, the matches placed representatives of two well-defined groups in Indian society in direct competition — where the winning group carried out certain rituals and the losing group became the sacrifice victims.

The Cenote of the Sacrifices

Another structure at Chichén-Itzá indicates a custom of sacrifices. A paved avenue, which starts at the Castillo and goes north for almost one thousand feet, leads to the Cenote (well) of the Sacrifices. This circular natural well seems man-made. It has a diameter of two hundred feet and its walls rise sixty-five feet above the greenish water. In pre-Columbian times, this cenote was a famous pilgrims' shrine. The vestiges of a steam bath on its edge testify that sacrifices were probably accompanied by purification rites. Bishop de Landa writes: "They (the Itzá) had and have had the custom of throwing live men in these wells in sacrifice to the gods in periods of drought; they believed that the victims did not die, even though they no longer saw them."

In 1562, despite the Spanish occupation, there were still signs of human sacrifices at the Chichén-Itzá cenote. The mayor of Madrid, Diego Sarmiento de Figueroa, on his visit to the Yucatán in the sixteenth century, wrote: "The gentlemen and main dignitaries of the town had the custom, after sixty days of fasting and abstinence, of going to the cenote at dawn and throwing in Indian women who belonged to each of the above-mentioned gentlemen and dignitaries. They (the women) had to ask the gods for a favorable year for their master. . . . The women, who were thrown in the water without being

bound, fell with all their weight, making a great din. At the end of the day, those who were still able to shout did so, and a rope was let down to them. When they reappeared, more dead than alive, fires were lit around them and copal incense was burnt. When the women regained their senses, they said that many persons were down there from their town who had welcomed them warmly. When they tried to raise their heads to look at them, however, they got strong knocks on the head; when they bent their heads under the water they thought they saw great abysses and holes, and those, the inhabitants of the depths, answered their questions about the good and bad year. . . ."

Between 1904 and 1907, an American named Edward Thompson undertook a dredging of the Chichén-Itzá cenote, and even explored it in a diving suit. Besides numerous engraved jade, stone, gold and copper objects, he found many flint knives and several skeletons: thirteen male and eight female, and twenty skeletons of children from eighteen months to eleven years old. The barbarous ritual of throwing human beings down the cenote was probably of Toltec origin, but various objects found at the bottom of the well belonged to the classical Mayan

Chichén-Itzá: The Caracol ("snail"). This is the only circular edifice in all of northern Mayan territory. Its tower was used as an astronomical observatory.

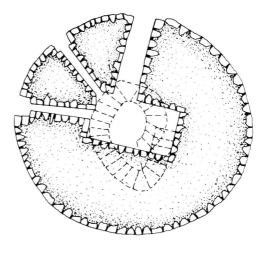

Chichén Viejo: Palace of the Nuns. The facade, entirely covered with stone decorations, is an example of the "Chenes" artistic style of the northern Maya.

Chichén-Itzá: Plan of the observation room in the Caracol, with the spiral staircase and the three openings oriented in precise astronomical directions.

period. One fragment of jade bears a date that corresponds to A.D. 706; its style is reminiscent of the site, Piedras Negras, in Petén. Another piece came from Palenque. These objects could indicate that in the seventh and eighth centuries the classical Maya made pilgrimages to the Chichén-Itzá cenote, coming from areas as far away as Petén, Chiapas, and the Usumacinta River, but it also could indicate that the objects were simply family belongings, passed on from generation to generation, or were products of exchange and trade. A definitive explanation should come from further excavations, particularly from a study of the monuments in the southern part of Chichén-Itzá — beyond the civil cenote that supplied the town with water.

The "Caracol" and Chichén Viejo

Several hundred feet south of the heart of Chichén-Itzá, a circular construction known as the "Caracol" (or snail) dominates the last series of Toltec structures found at this site. This is the only structure of its kind in Mayan territory — a style reserved in a later period for the temples of the wind god in central Mexico.

The Caracol owes its name to an interior spiral staircase which leads to a small observation room at the top. The edifice is a sort of tower four hundred feet high, resting on two terraces set one upon the other. Through three openings in the walls of the tower, ancient Mayan astronomers must have scrutinized the heavens.

Beyond the Caracol, typical classical Mayan structures emerge, and the city of Toltec invaders is left behind. Here, in Chichén Viejo, there are roof combs, facades with stone decorations, and masks of Chac, the Mayan rain god, with his long "elephant trunk" nose, above the doors and on the friezes. In the building called "Akab D'zib," which means "obscure writing," a typical bas-relief stone panel of the Mayan classical period depicts a priest seated on a throne opposite a container and surrounded by glyphs. Another lintel, part of an edifice in the Group of the Date, shows a hieroglyphic inscription of the Long Count,

Left:
Chichén Viejo: La Iglesia. The facades of this edifice show tendencies toward geometric forms, typical of the "Puuc" artistic style of the northern Maya.

or "initial series," that describes the date "10.2.9.1.9.9. Muluc 7 Zac," which corresponds to A.D. 879. This date indicates that Mayan populations inhabited Chichén-Itzá long before the arrival of the first Toltec invaders. In the light of certain passages in the *Books of Chilam Balam* and recent archaeological research conducted in the Yucatán, some scholars surmise that two waves of migration, originating in Petén, occurred in the Yucatán during the Mayan classical period. In their wake, it is suggested that the Maya founded ten "provincial" classical cities, far from the great centers in Petén and Chiapas, and far from their original cultural influences.

The foundation of Chichén-Itzá is referred to in various parts of the different versions of the *Books of Chilam Balam*. Thus, in one section of the *Chilam Balam of Chumayel* it says: "During the katun 6 Ahau (from A.D. 435–455) the discovery of Chichén-Itzá occurred." The *Chilam Balam of Mani* sets the founding in A.D. 455. As for the *Chronicle of Tizimin*, it says: "It happened that Chichén-Itzá came to our knowledge in katun 8 Ahau (A.D. 416–435)." The date 879, inscribed on the stone of the Chichén Viejo lintel, is the last date inscribed on a classical monument in the Yucatán. From then on, some form of foreign influence, such as Toltec, was evident in the structures and art of the Mayan world.

Below:
Chichén Viejo: Corners of La Iglesia and
the Palace of the Nuns. The two large stone
masks attached to the corners of the two
buildings show an elongated nose. These
are representations of Chac, the god of rain.

The Chenes and Puuc Styles

Before taking leave of Chichén-Itzá, we should consider two build-ings, both minor but with facades that represent two special styles of Mayan architecture in the Yucatán. In most classical sites, the facades of buildings are decorated with modeled stucco. Only rarely was stone used for decorative effects. But in the architectural style known as *Chenes*, stone decoration replaces the stucco. An example of this at Chichén-Itzá is the so-called Palace of the Nuns, and we shall be seeing more buildings with the *Chenes* style. The other particular style, the *Puuc* style, is characterized by a tendency toward geometric forms; in certain buildings using the *Puuc* style, the columns are made smooth up to the capitals. The facade of La Iglesia at Chichén-Itzá demonstrates the *Puuc* style, although the columns do not appear to have such clean lines.

Mayapán

The site of Mayapán, in the northwestern region of the Yucatán, is a fortress-type center which was apparently completed by Kukulkán before he left the Yucatán for good. Before departing, however, he supposedly placed the Cocom dynasty, a noble Toltec family, on the throne of Mayapán.

The histories of the Cocom dynasty and the Xiu dynasty, which settled Uxmal, were somewhat similar. Both Cocom and Xiu were probably from the north and spoke Toltec, but it seems that most of the men under them spoke the Mayan tongue and came from Tabasco. They were perhaps the descendants of the first Mayan emigrants who were said to have founded ten colonial cities in the Yucatán during the classical period (around the fifth century).

The position of the three dynasties in this region (including that of Chichén-Itzá), was relatively fragile, and they decided to form a triple alliance. Mayan sources say that between 987 and 1185 the Mayapán League was founded, by means of which the three leaders of Chichén-Itzá, Uxmal and Mayapán jointly governed the surrounding lands in peace and prosperity for two centuries. (Archaeological evidence tends to dispute this somewhat, however, because it reveals that Uxmal was deserted during part of the two centuries involved.)

At the end of the twelfth century, the Mayan texts then say, the power of Chichén-Itzá began to overshadow Mayapán, and a Mayapán leader, Hunac Ceel, also called Cauich, decided to take the destiny of his people in hand. Knowing that he had no rights to rulership under the strict cultural rules of hierarchy, he undertook an unusual step to the throne.

As the *Book of Chilam Balam of Chumayel* relates: The Mayapán authorities organized a pilgrimage one day to the çenote at Chichén-Itzá. Many people were thrown down the well on this occasion, and the spectators waited to see whether one of the victims would emerge to the surface to tell the gods' answer concerning the best way to administer Mayapán. When none of the victims surfaced, Hunac Ceel quickly dove into the water of the well, returned to the surface and shouted to the populace that he had spoken with the gods. The gods told him, he said, that from that moment on he should be the king of the entire Yucatán peninsula. Brought out of the well, he was then proclaimed Lord of Mayapán and of all the cities of the Yucatán. He made Mayapán a powerful and feared city, it is said, by calling on Mexican mercenaries (*Ah canul* — "protectors"), to assist him. These men were expert archers and introduced the bow and arrow to the Yucatán. The Comom dynasty reigned in the Yucatán for 250 years until 1441, it is said, when Ah Xupan Xiu from Uxmal gathered together the other leaders of the peninsula to destroy Mayapán and kill its chief and his sons.

A Real City

It would be difficult to confirm the above-described historical accounts through an examination of the archaeological evidence at Mayapán. At first glance, little of the site seems to indicate the important role the city must have played in the centuries preceding the Spanish Conquest. The monuments do not even allow a comparison with those of Uxmal and Chichén-Itzá.

THE RISE OF HUNAC CEEL TO POWER

Then began the introduction of tribute to them at Chichén. At Tikuch arrived the tribute of the four men. 11 Ahau was the name of the katun when the tribute was handled. There at Cetelac it was assembled; there it was. Then came the tribute of Holtun Zuiua, there at Cetelac, where they agreed in their opinions. 13 Ahau was the name of the katun when the head-chiefs received the tribute.

Then began their reign; then began their rule. Then they began to be served; then those who were to be thrown into the cenote arrived; then they began to throw them into the well that their prophecy might be heard by their rulers. Their prophecy did not come. It was Cauich, Hunac Ceel, Cauich was the name of the man there, who put out his head at the opening of the well on the south side. Then he went to take it. Then he came forth to declare the prophecy. Then began the taking of the prophecy. Then began his prophecy. Then they began to declare him ruler. Then he was set in the seat of the rulers by them. Then they began to declare him head-chief. He was not the ruler formerly; that was only the office of Ah Mex Cuc. Now the representative of Ah Mex Cuc was declared ruler. The eagle, they say, was his mother. Then, they say, he was sought on his hill. Then they began to take the prophecy of this ruler after it was declared. Then they began to set aloft the house on high for the ruler. Then began the construction of the stairway. Then he was set in the house on high in 13 Ahau, the sixth reign. Then began the hearing of the prophecy, of the news, of the setting up of Ah Mex Cuc, as he was called. Then he carried nearly to Baca the news of Ah Mex Cuc. He was placed there. Then he began to be treated as a lord; then obedience to the name of Ah Mex Cuc began. Then he was obeyed; then he was served there at the mouth of the well. Chichén-Itzam was its name because the Itzá went there. Then he removed the stones of the land, the stones of the sowed land, the place of Itzam, and they went into the water. Then began the introduction of misery there at Chichén-Itzá. Then he went to the east and arrived at the home of Ah Kin Coba.

The Book of Chilam Balam of Chumayel (pp. 74–76)

Mayapán: Incense burner representing the rain god with his forked tongue and "serpent" nose. He holds in his right hand the cup of water that will send rain to the earth; in his left hand he holds a human heart, evoking the germination of maize.

In 1950, an archaeological team from the Carnegie Institution of Washington undertook an excavation in Mayapán, discovering that the city covers a much larger area than had been imagined. They found, in fact, that 3,600 constructions lie inside the bastions, including a religious enclosure referred to by Bishop de Landa, rectangular palaces whose colonnades open onto paved plazas, and habitations so closely aligned that common walls exist between some of them. A great wall surrounds the city, within which according to Bishop de Landa, the head-chiefs of the neighboring states lived.

Mayapán was apparently not like the other Mayan sites — primarily a ceremonial center. Rather, this was a real city with a population of about ten thousand persons. Like medieval European cities, it was an administrative and political center and served as a refuge and fortress. Very few of the buildings can be regarded as religious in function, and most of the latter form a small ceremonial center surrounded by residential mounds.

Following an analysis of excavation reports, the Mayan scholar J. Eric S. Thompson stressed the cultural poverty of the Mayapán military regime. The serpentine columns, round structures, pillars, and bas-reliefs at Mayapán were essentially Toltec-inspired, and were pallid imitations of what was created at Chichén-Itzá. Jade ornaments, polychrome pottery, and artistic objects have not been found. Rather, the tombs of the leaders reveal traces of the massacres that must have taken place during funeral rites. In one of the tombs, forty-one skeletons surround one skeleton, who appears to have been the master.

The mediocrity of Mayapán's architecture, in general, is a confirmation of this city's preoccupation with power and war. Undressed rough blocks of stone were used, covered up crudely with heavy overlays of stucco. Short colonnades stood alone, unattached to temples, lacking the corbel vaulting that was so typical of the classical Maya structures.

The pottery in Mayapán was degenerate, becoming decidedly coarse in the fourteenth century. Mass-produced censers reveal a lack of religious feeling, probably due to the predominance of a warrior cast and a functionary class over the priests; the walls of the aristocratic houses are of better quality than the temple walls. Burned beams, broken altars, smashed censers, and heaped-up skeletons with flint spear points still in their bones — all bear witness to the tone of this city.

Mayapán: View of the city center. Archaeological excavations carried out in this city serve only to emphasize its architectural mediocrity. But for centuries this center apparently oppressed the entire Yucatán peninsula with its power.

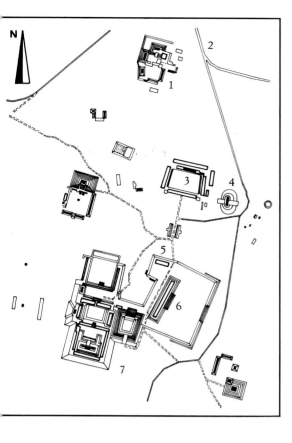

Uxmal: General plan.
1. North Group
2. Road to Mérida
3. The Quadrangle of
   the Nunnery
4. Pyramid of the
   Soothsayer
5. The House of Turtles
6. The Governor's Pal-
   ace
7. South Group

On the following pages:
Uxmal: General view. At the left, a part of the Quadrangle of the Nunnery. At the right, Pyramid of the Soothsayer.

Uxmal

According to the *Chilam Balam of Mani*: "During the *katun 2 Ahau* (from 987 to 1007) Ah Zuitok Xiu took up residence at Uxmal." Uxmal means "thrice built," a name that suggests that the city must have been founded much earlier than the arrival of the Xiu described above. Rather, it was apparently established by the first Mayan emigrants coming from Petén — supposedly around the fifth century.

For the visitor imbued with the history and architecture of the other Yucatán centers that were inspired by the Toltecs, (Chichén-Itzá or Mayapán), the overall view of Uxmal is surprising. There is no doubt about the authentically Mayan imprint of Uxmal, but it is nevertheless difficult to establish relationships between the buildings of Uxmal and those of classical Mayan cities. The cultural style of the classical Maya, apparently exported from the fifth century on by the wave of colonizing emigrants who invaded the Yucatán peninsula, seems to have undergone gradual changes during the centuries. The custom of erecting stelae every twenty years died out, hieroglyphic inscriptions became rare, and calendars were reduced to the maximum of simplicity. On the other hand, the decorative stucco motifs that modestly adorned the facades of a number of temples in the ancient cities became more prevalent, were stylized, and were repeated over and over to the extent that they covered all the facades. The corbel vault (described in detail in a later chapter) remained in its immutable form, however, and roof combs continued to crown the temples.

Nothing is known today of what happened to the cities of the Yucatán between the ninth and the eleventh centuries. According to the *Books of Chilam Balam*, the descendants of the Mayan emigrants abandoned the Yucatán at that time to settle in Tabasco, at Chakanputun (present-day Champoton). The Toltecs, in their march of conquest toward the south, appear to have brought these Mayan descendants along with them, who thereby returned toward Petén — their land of origin. Meanwhile, as the Toltecs spread the cult of the Plumed Serpent and the custom of human sacrifices throughout the Yucatán, they also spread the usages, beliefs, language, writing and calendars of the Maya.

Because of a lack of precise historical data, the terms "Maya of the North," or "renaissance Maya," refer to the peninsula Mayans who lived under Toltec rule. Uxmal was, in reality, the artistic capital of the complex of cities in the Yucatán. Here and there non-Mayan influences are evident in the architecture and in decorations, but they are modest. Like the three ancient codices of the Yucatán and the *Books of Chilam Balam*, Uxmal is essentially Mayan; it succeeded in freeing itself from much of the Toltec influence.

The Buildings

The site of Uxmal extends over an area about one-half mile in length and six hundred yards in width. It is made up of various architectural groupings, of which the three principal ones have been explored and restored in part. Each of the groups is placed in a highly precise manner: the Pyramid of the Soothsayer (or the Magician) in a vertical line, the Quadrangle of the Nunnery in a square, and the Governor's Palace in a horizontal line.

Five superimposed temples, one virtually embedded in the other, make up the Pyramid of the Soothsayer, which is a synthesis in stone of three centuries of continual occupation. Each of the succeeding temples buried the preceding one, and thereby altered the orientation of the sanctuary. Temple IV is in the *Chenes* (Campeche) style. A mask of the Mayan rain god Chac decorates the facade. The god's jaw acts as an entrance — an obvious reference to the function of the temple for the "passage" rites. (According to the Mayan texts, one must die in the jaws of the god in order to be reborn to a new life, which follows initiation.) But this type of facade decoration is unexpected in Uxmal, which is generally of the *Puuc* (Yucatán) style. Decoration on the upper part of the facade only is an essential characteristic of the *Puuc* style; another characteristic is the presence of molding, at the top and under the decorated portion.

One enters the Quadrangle of the Nunnery, which stands on a platform in front of the Pyramid of the Soothsayer, by means of a stairway built on the southern side. Aside from its own architectural

THE CHALLENGE TO PLAY THE GAME

The messengers of Hun-Camé and Vucub-Camé arrived immediately.

"Go, Ahpop Achih!" they were told. "Go and call Hun-Hunahpú and Vucub-Hunahpú. Say to them, 'Come with us. The lords say that you must come.' They must come here to play ball with us so that they shall make us happy, for really they amaze us. So, then, they must come," said the lords. "And have them bring their playing gear, their rings, their gloves, and have them bring their rubber balls, too," said the lords. "Tell them to come quickly," they told the messengers.

And these messengers were owls: Chabi-Tucur, Huracán-Tucur, Caquix-Tucur and Holom-Tucur. These were the names of the messengers of Xibalba.

Chabi-Tucur was swift as an arrow; Huracán-Tucur had only one leg; Caquix-Tucur had a red back, and Holom-Tucur had only a head, no legs, but he had wings. . . . The owl messengers went directly to the ball-court and delivered their message exactly as it was given to them. . . .

"Did the Lords Hun-Camé and Vucub-Camé really say that we must go with you?"

"They certainly said so, and 'Let them bring all their playing gear,' the lords said.". . . .

Hun-Hunahpú and Vucub-Hunahpú went immediately and the messengers took them on the road. Thus they were descending the road to Xibalba, by some very steep stairs. They went down until they came to the bank of a river which flowed rapidly between the ravines called Nuziván cul and Cuziván, and crossed it. Then they crossed the river which flows among thorny calabash trees. There were very many calabash trees, but they passed through them without hurting themselves.

Then they came to the bank of a river of blood and crossed it without drinking its waters; they only went to the river bank and so they were not overcome. They went on until they came to where four roads joined, and there at the crossroads they were overcome.

One of the four roads was red, another black, another white, and another yellow. And the black road said to them: "I am the one you must take because I am the way of the Lord." So said the road.

And from here on they were already overcome. They were taken over the road to Xibalba and when they arrived at the countil room of the Lords of Xibalba, they had already lost the match.

POPOL VUH
(pp. 112–113)

Uxmal: Pyramid of the Soothsayer. A long series of Chac masks decorates the ramp along the side of the great stairway.

THE DEFEAT AT THE GAME

Well, the first ones who were seated there were only figures of wood, arranged by the men of Xibalba. These they greeted first:

"How are you, Hun-Camé?" they said to the wooden man. "How are you, Vucab-Camé?" they said to the other wooden man. But they did not answer. Instantly the Lords of Xibalba burst into laughter and all the other lords began to laugh loudly, because they already took for granted the downfall and defeat of Hun-Hunahpú and Vucub-Hunahpú. And they continued to laugh.

Then Hun-Camé and Vucub-Camé spoke: "Very well," they said. "You have come. Tomorrow you shall prepare the mask, your rings, and your gloves," they said.

"Come and sit down on our bench," they said. But the bench which they offered them was of hot stone, and when they sat down they were burned. They began to squirm around on the bench, and if they had not stood up they would have burned their seats.

The Lords of Xibalba burst out laughing again; they were dying of laughter; they writhed from pain in their stomach, in their blood, and in their bones, caused by their laughter, all the Lords of Xibalba laughed.

"Go now to that house," they said. "There you will get your sticks of fat pine and your cigar and there you shall sleep."

Immediately they arrived at the House of Gloom. There was only darkness within the house. Meanwhile the Lords of Xibalba discussed what they should do.

"Let us sacrifice them tomorrow, let them die quickly, quickly, so that we can have their playing gear to use in play," said the Lords of Xibalba to each other.

Well, their fat-pine sticks were round and were called zaquitoc, which is the pine of Xibalba. Their fat-pine sticks were pointed and filed and were as bright as bone; the pine of Xibalba was very hard.

Hun-Hunahpú and Vucub-Hunahpú entered the House of Gloom. There they were given their fat-pine sticks, a single lighted stick which Hun-Camé and Vucub-Camé sent them, together with a lighted cigar for each of them which the lords had sent. They went to give them to Hun-Hunahpú and Vucub-Hunahpú.

They found them crouching in the darkness when the porters arrived with the fat-pine sticks and the cigars. As they entered, the pine sticks lighted the place brightly.

"Each of you light your pine sticks and your cigars; come and bring them back at dawn, you must not burn them up, but you must return them whole; this is what the lords told us to say." So they said. And so they were defeated. They burned up the pine sticks, and they also finished the cigars which had been given to them.

POPOL VUH
(pp. 113–116)

value, the quadrangle is interesting because of the orientation of the edifices at four cardinal points and because of the contents of the facade friezes. Unfortunately, scholars know nothing of the function of this complex, as is the case with the Governor's Palace, to be described later. The Spaniards gave the name Nunnery to this group of buildings because the many rooms reminded them of the convent cells in Spain.

A number of questions come to mind when one begins an examination of these edifices. Among them: Is the number of openings in the facades linked to the orientation of the edifices?

The southern edifice in the quadrangle, like the other three, opens onto an inner courtyard (213 × 258 feet), which is entered by traversing a vaulted gateway cut into the heart of the edifice. Eight rooms open onto the patio, facing north, and another eight face south on the other side of the edifice. A small stone hut, in a form typical of the common habitation of this region, crowns each entrance. A rich decoration of feathers supplants the roof straw, and is in turn surmounted by a mask of Chac. The opening of each hut is carved in the form

Uxmal: Pyramid of the Soothsayer. A passageway set at the top of the stairway on the back side of the pyramid leads to the five structures inside built before this one.

Uxmal: Plan of the Pyramid of the Soothsayer.

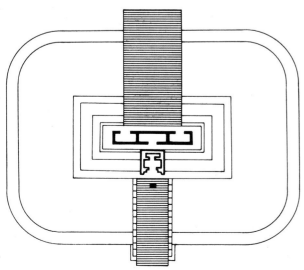

of a niche, but none of the statues that must have once stood in them has ever been found.

Squarely in front of the vaulted passage stands the northern edifice, the most important structure of the Quadrangle of the Nunnery. A wide stairway ninety feet long, flanked by two diminutive temples, leads to this structure. The one on the left is called the Temple of Venus because some of Uxmal's first visitors held that the facade contained a motif symbolizing that planet.

The northern edifice is long and contains thirteen double rooms. Eleven entrances lead into the patio which faces south, and another two open onto the side facades, to the east and to the west respectively. Above each opening a frieze alternates a realistic hut with a roof of feathers and a two-headed serpent, and four masks of Chac, super-imposed and adorned with an enormous mask of the Mexican god of rain, Tlaloc, decorated with the symbol of the year of Teotihuacan. Between the huts and the masks of Chac, various motifs fill in the spaces: frets, stylized serpents, small columns, and human figures, among others.

The eastern edifice is the simplest and best preserved structure of the four. It presents five openings onto five inner halls, with the central hall and its entrance larger than the others. Each of the halls opens onto the central patio. The frieze on this structure, cut on a background of stones in cross-vault style, represents six motifs consisting of eight rectilineal two-headed serpents laid out in a parallel line, one over the other. This lattice pattern flares elegantly upward to the top of the

Uxmal: Quadrangle of the Nunnery. Eastern edifice. The frieze on this building, the simplest and best preserved structure in the complex, has a background of cross-vaulted stone with six motifs of eight two-headed serpents.

building, where the head of an owl with a headdress of additional feathers is inserted in the upper part. Stylized masks of Chac decorate the corners of the facade and the area over the main entrance.

The seven entrances of the western edifice look toward the east. The central door and hall are exceptionally large. The ornamental motif is an imposing throne bearing a personage with the head of an old man and the body of a turtle, protected by a canopy. Modest thrones without personages dominate the two entrances nearby, and the next to last group of doors is adorned with a vertical line of three masks of Chac, like the corners of the facades. The hut motif, once again, appears above the first and the last doors.

On the frieze, two plumed serpents, laid down in the form of a spiral column around each throne, reach out at each end toward the corners of the facade; the head of a personage appears in their open jaws. Other sculptures embedded into the frieze depict naked individuals with tattooed genitals (an authentically Toltec motif, like the Plumed Serpent). Some specialists assert that these decorations were inserted into the work long after its construction, which was apparently completed before the arrival of the Toltecs — approximately at the end of the classical period or perhaps a few decades later (about A.D. 900).

Two cultures must have cohabitated in the quadrangle, with the Mayan culture predominating. The Plumed Serpent motif frames the three thrones of this edifice, after all, symbolizing what must have happened in the Yucatán, probably beginning with the end of the tenth century. The Mayan world, aroused from a long torpor, resumed the religious and artistic activities that were typical of it, while also fitting into the scheme of the Toltecs. In addition, there are the other representations of the god Tlaloc on the northern edifice, on the two small temples at the foot of its stairway, and, more particularly, on the columns and the frieze of the temple of Venus, which unquestionably bear a Toltec imprint.

The Governor's Palace is one of the most beautiful buildings in pre-Columbian America. It is of such prodigious proportions that the Spaniards themselves thought that only a "governor" could live in such a dwelling — thus naming it. It dates from about A.D. 900 — the same as the Nunnery.

It is 318 feet long. Like the buildings of the Quadrangle of the Nunnery, it rests on a vast terrace overlooking the city. It is made up of a central edifice and two side structures, which were originally separated from the palace by a vaulted gateway, making it possible to go from one side of the building to the other without going around it. Later on, the two complementary buildings were separated by a transversal wall with two small cells preceded by porticoes and columns built on each side of the wall.

The main facade of the Governor's Palace faces the east; it has eleven entrances, including those of the annexes. A flared motif in the form of a capital dominates the central opening — similar to that of the Nunnery. Rising out of a background of eight two-headed serpents, a semicircular throne bears a personage in badly mutilated stone, crowned with an extravagant headdress of feathers.

The frieze, a splendid decoration, ten feet high, runs around the entire palace. Its 2,200 square feet of surface indicate the innumerable technical difficulties that its creators must have faced. The theme of the cross vault, making up the motif of the frieze, is comprised of twenty thousand identical carved stones, each weighing several pounds. There are also one hundred and fifty masks of Chac (three feet long, almost two feet high), numerous stylized serpents and altogether more than twenty thousand different carved stones placed tightly together.

How, then, did the Maya reach such a high degree of specialization in the art of construction? For the creation of this masterpiece required workmanship of incredible precision. It could possibly have been an aspect of Toltec influence, but it seems to be that a typically Mayan framework provides a clue. That framework is the Río Bec style, which

Left
Uxmal: Quadrangle of the Nunnery. Detail from the eastern edifice. The central entranceway, surmounted by a frieze representing three overlaid masks of Chac, is larger than the others.

On the following pages:
Uxmal: Quadrangle of the Nunnery. Northern edifice, extending on a platform 325 feet long. This is the most important structure in the complex, which includes four edifices closed up so as to form a quadrangle.

Above:
Uxmal: Detail from one facade on the northern edifice of the Quadrangle of the Nunnery. Protruding noses, globular eyes, decorated eyebrows, grinning mouths decorated with fangs, and atrophied (or even non-existent) jaws characterize the four Chac masks on this facade.

Left:
Uxmal: Quadrangle of the Nunnery. The north corner of the eastern edifice. The elongated noses belonging to the five Chac masks set on this corner are missing.

Uxmal: Reconstruction of the Quadrangle of the Nunnery.

derives its name from the vicinity of the Bec River near Petén. This style is characterized primarily by towers and temples built in a *trompe l'oeil* form, gigantic masonry scenes that attempt to imitate the buildings of Tikal; it is here that the evolution from stucco decorations to stone decorations appears to have taken place. In order to increase the resistance of the stucco bas-reliefs, the Río Bec Maya used pieces of stone that protruded from the facades and served as supports for the molding. These stone supports, which became more and more numerous, ended up forming mosaics, whereas the molding itself began to disappear from the facades.

The Mask of Chac

The mask of the rain god Chac, an essential decorative motif of the Mayan monuments of the Yucatán, is repeated an infinite number of times on the facades of the buildings at Uxmal. The nose extends forward in the form of a proboscis, the globular eyes peer out beneath decorated eyebrows, the ears are surmounted by horns, the sneering, half-open mouth exposes jutting fangs, and the mandible is emaciated.

This mask of Chac is omnipresent in Mayan architecture. It reaches out along the friezes, fills in the corners, and clings to the space above doors. Even today Indians of the Mayan tongue in the Yucatán venerate the god Chac. Eight consecutive months of drought in an arid land devoid of rivers explains the survival of this divinity. (The features of Chac on the Mayan facades presents many affinities with the Chinese *t'ao t'ie* mask of the Chang period, (1523-1028 B.C.), and it is tempting to search for some relationship between them — despite the intervention of two thousand years.)

Traces of this mask have been found in several of the classical cities — among them at Uaxactún, a small city near Tikal, and at Tikal itself. At Uaxactún, Sylvanus G. Morley discovered the E VII sub-structure,

where great stucco masks decorated the ramps of the stairways leading to the platform on which a wooden temple had once rested. This structure was considered at the time the most ancient in the entire Mayan area. Some of the characteristics of the masks later found on the Yucatán facades were also to be seen at Uaxactún: decorated eyebrows, emaciated mandibles, and yawning jaws giving a glimpse of fangs.

At Tikal, inside Edifice 5 D-33, archaeologists have brought to light a platform supporting a temple decorated with masks, and also a structure (33 RD) built in approximately A.D. 460 which is flanked by two colossal stucco masks depicting the god with the long nose. This is a monumental replica of the god of rain, represented in the codices with the features of a long-nosed personage whose face was narrowed down like the head of a serpent. Archaeologists at Tikal have also discovered in Tomb 195, (A.D. 600), three wooden statues of the rain god coated with stucco; the stylized countenance calls to mind the head of a serpent. But Chac, the god with the long nose, dispenser of rain, whose features are often identified with those of the serpent, appears to combine with the form of a jaguar when representing the four *bacab* that support the celestial vault. It was in the jaguar-serpent association that the mask invaded the facades of the Yucatán.

The House of Turtles

A sobriety of line and balanced proportions make the House of Turtles (ninety feet long, thirty-one feet wide, twenty feet high) one of the best built monuments in the Yucatán. Its elegance even calls to mind classical Greek temples. This edifice owes its name to a sequence of small turtles on a tablet applied to the cornice molding. Rather than a temple, this House of the Turtles appears to be a civil building, in that it was not erected on a pyramid.

A number of authors point out that the turtle, because of its amphibious nature, could have been linked to the Mayan water cult. But neither the texts, nor the codices, nor the iconography, nor even ethnography seems to call attention to such a relationship. In the texts referring to the Maya, as in the Toltec iconography, there is virtually no information regarding this animal. In the *Madrid Codex*, the turtle is connected with the planets and at times appears to represent the stars. The animal is linked with certain astronomical signs in this codex, and according to the German codice scholar Ernst Förstemann, the turtle is the symbol of solstices. However, it is highly unlikely that the House of the Turtles was an edifice set aside for astronomers.

Perhaps there is a link between the House of the Turtles and the stone statue, half-man and half-turtle, which is placed at the height of the first level of the frieze on the western edifice of the Quadrangle of the Nunnery. The statue faces the east, and opposite it, on the facade of the eastern edifice, the bust of an owl crowns the six two-headed serpents. The owl is the symbol of a clan mentioned in the *Popol Vuh*, the sacred book of the Quiché Maya of Guatemala (in the citation, "the owl ones" live at Xilbalbá, in the lower regions of Petén). Meanwhile, an owl also appears sculptured on the chest of a personage on a stele at Dos Pozos. It could be that the owl, which is not a well-known Mayan divinity, represents at Uxmal the emblem of a clan. The same conclusion could be reached for the turtle. The people of the owl clan perhaps occupied the eastern edifice, and the chieftain of the turtle clan was seated, surrounded by his retinue, in the western edifice. And, possibly, the clan of the turtle was also associated with a second edifice: the House of the Turtles. One might also think that this edifice had another function — relating to music. In the framework of the Mayan social organization, *Ah Popol* was the cantor in

There were many punishments in Xibalba; the punishments were of many kinds.

The first was the House of Gloom, Quequma-ha, in which there was only darkness.

The second was Xuxulim-ha, the house where everybody shivered, in which it was very cold. A cold, unbearable wind blew within.

The third was the House of Jaguars, Balami-ha, it was called, in which there were nothing but jaguars which stalked about, jumped around, roared, and made fun. The jaguars were shut up in the house.

Zotzi-há, the House of Bats, the fourth place of punishment was called. Within this house there were nothing but bats which squeaked and cried and flew around and around. The bats were shut in and could not get out.

The fifth was called Chayim-há, the House of Knives, in which there were only sharp, pointed knives, silent or grating against each other in the house.

There were many places of torture in Xibalba, but Hun-Hunahpú and Vucub-Hunahpú did not enter them. We only mention the names of these houses of punishment.

When Hun-Hunahpú and Vucub-Hunahpx came before Hun-Camé and Vucub-Camé, they said: "Where are my cigars? Where are my sticks of fat pine which I gave you last night?"

"They are all gone, Sir."

"Well. Today shall be the end of your days. Now you shall die. You shall be destroyed, we will break you into pieces and here your faces will stay hidden. You shall be sacrificed," said Hun-Camé and Vucub-Camé.

They sacrificed them immediately and buried them in the Pucbal-Chah, as it was called. Before burying them, they cut off the head of Hun-Hunahpú and buried the older brother together with the younger brother.

"Take the head and put it in that tree which is planted on the road," said Hun-Camé and Vucub-Camé. And having put the head in the tree, instantly the tree, which had never borne fruit before the head of Hun-Hunahpú was placed among its branches, was covered with fruit. And this calabash tree, it is said, is the one which we now call the head of Hun-Hunahpú.

Hun-Camé and Vucub-Camé looked in amazement at the fruit on the tree. The round fruit was every where; but they did not recognize the head of Hun-Hunahpú; it was exactly like the other fruit of the calabash tree. So it seemed to all of the people of Xibalba when they came to look at it.

According to their judgment, the tree was miraculous, because of what had instantly occurred when they put Hun-Hunahpú's head among its branches. And the Lords of Xibalba said:

"Let no one come to pick this fruit. Let no one come and sit under this tree!" they said, and so the Lords of Xibalba resolved to keep everybody away.

The head of Hun-Hunahpú did not appear again, because it had become one and the same as the fruit of the gourd tree. Nevertheless, a girl heard the wonderful story. Now we shall tell about her arrival.

POPOL VUH
(pp. 117–118)

charge of the dances and the musical instruments, and in each village he was also the master of the *popolna*, the house where the dances were worked up and where the musical instruments were stored. The shell of the turtle is a typically Mayan musical instrument, which appears in the hands of the musicians painted in the frescoes of Bonampak. (It is still used by the Mayan-speaking Indians in Guatemala.) In ancient times, as today in Guatemala, the instrument was made from the shell of fresh-water turtles. In Uxmal, which is so close to the sea, in a region where there are no streams, the turtles represented on the edifice are fresh-water turtles. Thus the House of the Turtles may have been the *popolna* of Uxmal.

Political and Social Organization

The accounts of the Maya set down by Spanish chroniclers give a rather precise idea of the life of that people, and are of great help in affording a better understanding of the enigmatic world of the classical and post-classical Maya. It must be remembered, however, that the Toltecs left a substantial imprint on the social and political affairs of the Yucatán Maya.

When the Spaniards arrived in the sixteenth century, two castes dominated the society of the Yucatán: the nobles and the priests. There was no rivalry between them. Or, rather, the politically powerful nobles had tremendous respect for the priests, who were the possessors of knowledge and who could deal with the gods. Beneath all these privileged persons were the mass of the people, and last, the slaves.

An explanation for some of the controversial facts in the civilization of the Yucatán must lie in the tacit accord between the priests and the nobles. Above all, the Toltec influence predominant in the cities of Chichén-Itzá and Mayapán reveals that in those two cities, at least, the priests (probably of Toltec origin) were at the service of their warrior chieftains, who belonged to the nobility. In other cities of the area, however — Uxmal, Kabah, and Sayil, for example — the caste of the nobility was largely Toltec and that of the priests Mayan. In these latter cities the priests appeared to hold sway over the cultural destiny of the people, with the tacit agreement, or perhaps even the support, of the nobles. These cities, then, were able to preserve their Mayan characteristics: inspired by the Mayan priests, built by the Mayan people, but socially organized by the Toltec nobility.

Each of the twenty states of the sixteenth-century Yucatán was dependent on a supreme chief, an *halach uinic* (or "true man"). This hereditary office was handed down from father to eldest son. If the latter was too young at the death of the father, paternal uncles assumed the regency. The *halach uinic* was a full-fledged king in his own territory, who was supposed to hold all power but not abuse it. His subjects referred to him as *Ahau*, which was equivalent to king, monarch, or emperor. It is interesting that this term had its original meaning in the calendars, being reserved for the last of the twenty days of the Mayan month — a day that had great importance in situating the time and dates in the Short Count (the time sequence supplanting the Long Count and used in the *Books of Chilam Balam*). This king, with the collaboration of the state council, made up of village chieftains, priests, and advisors, directed the domestic and foreign policies of the state. One of the king's fundamental missions, at the outset of a new *katun* (a period of twenty years) was to examine all those citizens who aspired to the post of village governor. The questioning, of a highly unusual nature, was conducted in an esoteric language. It is obvious that this language was set aside for a very small number of individuals, and in the final analysis the *halach uinic* always named his governors from the same privileged caste. Indications are that the

interrogation of the chiefs was the reflection of a rotation of powers — parallel to the rotation of time.

The Mayan hereditary nobility was called *almehenoob*, literally "those who have a father and mother," which is to say those who belong to a lineage. It was from this layer of society that the *halach uinic* recruited his governors, in keeping with the criterion of the questioning of the leaders. The governors (*bataboob*) were also judges. They made sure that the people observed the directives of the priests, and more especially, they kept watch over the agriculture, as dictated by the calendars. Their essential function consisted of verifying the punctuality and exactness of the tribute paid by the village to the king, and they were assisted in this task by delegates (*ah leloob*). In wartime the governors recruited the militia, who then went to place themselves at the orders of the great war chieftain, the *nacom*.

The post of war chieftain was hereditary, but the supreme commander was elected every three years. He had tremendous responsibilities, and was venerated like an idol. He received offerings of incense and was carried to the temple in a procession. On the other hand, he was called upon to lead an altogether exemplary life for the three years of his mandate, observing absolute chastity and a number of food taboos. The counselors, *ah cuch caloob*, served in twos or threes, hierarchically speaking, right after the governor. Without their con-

Uxmal: Quadrangle of the Nunnery. The eastern corner of the southern edifice. A rich decoration with a feather motif serves as the "thatch roof" of the decorative hut set on the corner of this facade. The molding enclosed in the lower part of the frieze is typical of the "Puuc" style.

Uxmal: Governor's Palace, set on a terrace
and measuring 318 feet in length. This is
often considered the most beautiful pre-
Columbian building in America.

sent, nothing could be done. Three of them, the *ah popol*, "those who are placed before the mat" (the mat is the symbol of authority) were entrusted with relations between the great lords and the common people. They were the chiefs of the *popolna*, the meeting houses where public affairs were discussed, and they were also the cantors responsible for music and dance.

At the head of all the priests was the supreme lord-serpent priest, (*Ahaucan*), who played a primary role in the diminutive states of the Yucatán. Highly respected by the nobility, he was distinguished by the fact that he had no one at his service. (He lived off offerings, which were often sumptuous).

The supreme priest was the first counselor of the chief of the territory, and the cultural destiny of the state depended on him. Sacrifices, divinations, the observation of the stars, the administration of the monasteries, teaching, chronological calculations, the drafting of codes: all these areas were his responsibility, including the construction of the holy cities, whose architectural composition he kept under rigid surveillance. He was assisted in these tasks by a large number of priests, the *ahkin*.

The omniscient Lord Serpent was the depository of the entire Mayan culture. Since the title was hereditary, knowledge was handed down from father to son and from generation to generation, seeming to survive any historical accidents that could have destroyed it. It is to these custodians of the traditions, in all probability highly theocratic at first, that we owe our knowledge of the Mayan cultural achievements. One category of priests, the *chilam*, specialized in divination and were highly respected by the Maya; when they appeared in public people ran up to them to lift them up to spare them from soiling themselves through contact with the ground.

Another leader in the hierarchy was a priest who was responsible for human sacrifices. For this reason he was held in little esteem. His specialty, and the fact that he bore the same name as that of the war chieftain, *nacom*, however, are proof of his Toltec origin. His four assistants, or *chaces*, were given the task of holding the human victims during the sacrifices; they were usually recruited among old men on the occasion of each ceremony.

On the lowest rung of the Mayan society were the slaves (*pentacoob*). Bishop de Landa reports that slavery was introduced into the Yucatán by the Cocom of Mayapán. Sylvanus Morley, however, contended that this custom existed with the Maya of the classical period; in support of his theory he mentioned the prisoners depicted in the bas-reliefs of the classical cities — those persons reduced to slavery for having lost a battle. At Dos Pozos, a person sculptured on a step of a stairway appears tied with a cord to an inscription, but nothing indicates definitely that he was a slave; the sculpture might very well commemorate a victory. In the frescoes of Bonampak, the prisoners seem destined for sacrifices rather than for slavery. The crouching men holding up the priests in the bas-reliefs in Palenque do appear to be slaves, but it is not easy to take a stand in this regard. Slavery did exist in the Yucatán, without doubt in the late period. The Spaniards adopted this practice, and they are depicted as trading slaves for wine.

There were five conditions that could make one a slave in the Mayan society of the Yucatán: one could be born a slave, be taken prisoner of war, be convicted of theft, be an orphan, or be sold by one's parents or by a tribal chieftain. The tariff of this commerce was one hundred cacao seeds for one slave — emphasizing the high commercial value of cacao and the low price of men in that society.

The People

An anonymous crowd of peasants and artisans helped to build Mayan society; an indefatigable and courageous people who labored for their own survival, paid tribute to the nobility and provided the

In this way the number of the twenty-four lords was completed and the twenty-four great houses came into being. Thus the grandeur and power of the sons of the Quiché grew, when they built the town of the ravines out of stone and mortar.

Then the small tribes and the great tribes came before the king. The Quiché increased when their glory and majesty waxed, when they raised the house of their gods and the house of their lords. But it was not they who worked, or constructed their houses either, or made the house of the gods, for they were made by their sons and vassals, who had multiplied.

And they were not cheating them, nor robbing them, nor seizing them by force, because in reality each belonged to the lords, and many of their brothers and relatives had come together and had assembled, to hear the commands of each of the lords.

The lords were really loved and great was their glory; and the sons and the vassals held the birthdays of the lords in great respect when the inhabitants of the country and the city multiplied.

But it did not happen that all the tribes delivered themselves up, and neither did the country and towns the inhabitants of them fall in battle, but instead they fell, because of the marvels of the lords, King Gucumatz and King Cotuhá. Gucumatz was truly a marvelous king. For seven days he mounted to the skies and for seven days he went down into Xibalba; seven days he changed himself into a snake and really became a serpent; for seven days he changed himself into an eagle; for seven days he became a jaguar; and his appearance was really that of an eagle and a jaguar. Another seven days he changed himself into clotted blood and was only motionless blood.

POPOL VUH
(*pp. 219-220*)

Uxmal: Two-headed jaguar in the form of a typical Mayan throne. This sculpture, situated opposite the Governor's Palace, is cut from one block of stone. It is thirty-nine inches long and twenty-four inches high.

Uxmal: Governor's Palace: Schematic drawing and plan. The two lateral vaulted doors divided the complex into three edifices.

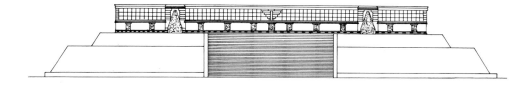

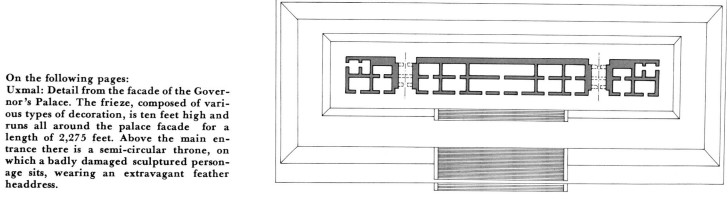

On the following pages:
Uxmal: Detail from the facade of the Governor's Palace. The frieze, composed of various types of decoration, is ten feet high and runs all around the palace facade for a length of 2,275 feet. Above the main entrance there is a semi-circular throne, on which a badly damaged sculptured personage sits, wearing an extravagant feather headdress.

Left:
Uxmal: Governor's Palace. A detail from
the frieze of the facade. A variety of twenty
thousand sculptured stone elements make up
the facade decoration.

RECOGNITION AS THE KING

Our early fathers and grandfathers tell
that the sun had already risen and the dawn
had appeared when the families of Gekaquch,
Zibakihay, Cavek, and Ahquehay were
formed. They had not wished to join Baqahol,
but the families had to suffer him when they
recognized him as their king. To hinder him,
they had said to him: "I will not receive you,
Baqahohl, although you have said, 'I am the
king.' Thus you spoke and you offered your
emerald to the mothers and the grandmothers.
Perhaps you named yourself king, Baqahol?
You are not our mother nor our grandmother."
But those who accepted him said: "He did
not say: 'I am your mother, I am your grandmother.' You are my king!" they said, and in
this manner they submitted to him.

As soon as they had recognized him as their
king and lord, they seated him in the chair
and on the throne, and afterwards they
bathed him in the bath with the pitcher and
the gourd. Then they gave him the mantle,
the girdle, the cradle, and they carried him,
they put the colored powders on him, and
the yellow stones, they annointed him with
soot and colored earth, and they gave him
the insignia of the kingdom in behalf of the
families and the clans. Thus our grandfathers
related, oh, my sons!

So it was that the families and the clans
recognized him whom they made their king.
So also did all the warriors in the place where
the dawn shone; and so was the seigniory constituted by the families and the clans.

They became numerous in the place where
their sun rose. Three branches of our people
saw the dawn there, the Zotzils, the Cakchiquels, and the Tukuchés.

The Annals of the Cakchiquels
(pp. 79-80)

offerings that left the priests free to think and to pray. The people
were capable and strong, and posterity is indebted to them for the
practical application of the priests' and the chiefs' architectural ideals.
It was up to the people to transport stones from the quarries and to
carve them with rudimentary neolithic tools. The exceptional mastery
of both materials and styles is indeed amazing.

In their planting of maize, the peasants knew only the methods of a
remote prehistoric period. Even today there are some half a million
descendants of the Maya still living in the barren Yucatán peninsula,
using the same archaic farming methods. Essentially they still worship
the same rain gods, lords of their agricultural destiny, and they continue to evince incredible energy and ingenuity in their handicrafts.

Right:
Uxmal: Governor's Palace. Entrance to the
vaulted corridor that originally led to the
other side of the edifice. The corridor was
later closed off by a transverse wall per-
mitting the construction of two small cells
preceded by columned porticoes.

Uxmal: House of the Turtles. The sober line and balanced proportions of this edifice make it one of the best-constructed in the Yucatán (ninety feet long, thirty-one feet wide, and twenty feet high).

SPIRIT OF THE VOLCANO

There, in the center of the Volcano of Fuego was the guardian of the road by which they arrived and which had been made by Zaquicoxol. "Who is the boy that we see?" they said. At once they sent Qoxahil and Qobakil, who went to observe and to use their magic power. And when they returned, they said that certainly his aspect was fearful, but he was only one and not many. Thus they said. "Let us go and see who it is that frightens you," said Gagavitz and Zactecauh. And when they had seen him, they said to him: "Who are you? Now we shall kill you. Why do you guard the road?" they said to him. And he answered: "Do not kill me. I live here, I am the spirit of the volcano." Thus he said. And immediately he begged for something with which to clothe himself. "We will give thee thy garment" they said. At once they gave him the garment: the wig, a breastplate the color of blood, sandals the color of blood, this was what Zaquicoxol received. In this manner he was saved. He departed and descended to the foot of the mountain.

They were disturbed then because of the trees and the birds. In truth they heard the trees speak, and the birds called to each other whistling there above them. And hearing them, they exclaimed: "What is this that we hear? Who are you?" they said. But it was only the noise of the trees; it was those who screech in the forest, the tigers and the birds that whistled. For this reason the name Chitabal was given to that place.

The Annals of the Cakchiquels
(pp. 61–62)

Uxmal: Plan of the House of the Turtles. The construction owes its name to the stone turtles that decorate the cornice.

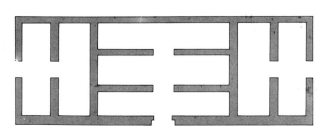

Kabah

An eight-mile pre-Columbian road links Uxmal with the site of Kabah. The existence of such a *sacbe* (literally "artificial road") does not mean that the Maya possessed means of locomotion, or of any kind of vehicle; they did not even use draft animals. It means, rather, that the roads were built for ritual and political reasons. Mayan roads, constructed with calcareous stones covered with cement (*sahcab*) were generally fourteen feet wide and at certain points rose up from two feet to seven feet from the level of the ground. They were laid out in a straight line — some only a few hundred feet long built to connect two sanctuaries, as at Tikal; others covered a few hundred miles, such as the road linking Cobá and Yaxuná. Roads made the multicolored religious processions easier and facilitated the transportation of offerings from one city to the other.

Most of the architecture of Kabah is considered in the *Puuc* style of Mayan art — that of the northern Yucatán peninsula generally. Mosaic friezes of sky-serpent masks with hooked noses cover the facade of the palace. Other structures reveal the same veneer masonry that was typical on the buildings at Uxmal. The only signs of foreign influence here are two door jambs, bearing a date of about A.D. 879, that show figures with spear-throwers and close-fitting jackets of the more northern Mexican peoples.

The Mayan Corbel Vault

The corridor or "arch" marking the entrance to Kabah is one of the best examples of the often-seen architectural detail of Mayan structures: the corbel vault. The archway at Kabah may have been built to welcome the Lord Serpent (or *halach uinic*) of Uxmal on his visits to Kabah. (It seems that Uxmal was the mother city of Kabah, holding religious and political power over it.)

The Mayans used the corbel vault both in the construction of corridors and in buildings. The historical development of the vault to the true arch is an example of the ingenuity of man when confronted with the problems of gravity. In the early history of man, a "vault" was a disorderly mass of slightly moistened stones fitted together precisely, along with a supporting center between two pillars — originating perhaps in Asia Minor. In the Western world, the Romans brought about an architectural revolution when, thanks to the use of cement, they were able to broaden the primitive type of vault and use the true arch. From that moment on architects could enhance their buildings with internal spaces that had formerly been unthinkable.

The Maya also used cement in their vaults, but the amount of space the vaults covered was limited. There were no broad areas between the pillars. In Mayan buildings, the distance between two pillars never exceeded fifteen feet. The problem was that the Maya never discovered the keystone principle — that the central stone of an arch is indispensable in supporting the whole. Without cement, the Mayan vault would have collapsed. The stones — cut in long groove-and-tongue joints — did not remain in place on their own. Each stone was cut longer than the one below it, so that a heavier weight above would press down and hold the lower stone in place. Gradually the longer stones arched toward each other, forming a sort of vault. When the cement dried, it held all the stones suspended. (The Maya probably used a complicated system of poles to do their cementing).

In reality, the Mayan corbel vault was a false vault: it did not hold

On pages 150-151:
Kabah: "Codz Poop," also called Palace of Masks. A total of 250 stone masks of Chac, set one upon the other, embellish the facade of this building, which is 147 feet long and twenty feet high.

up the mass, but was itself held up by mass. Though brilliant architects, the Maya did not know how to take full advantage of the materials they used, and did not give their buildings the beautiful interiors one might have expected. The rooms in Mayan structures are small, narrow, and dark. The Mayas seem to have created the vault only as a symbolic form — evoking perhaps the interior of primitive temples that had walls of adobe and roofs of straw.

Kabah: "Codz Poop." Plan and schematic drawing showing the distribution of the Chac masks that decorate the facade.

The Codz Poop and the Gods

Two hundred and fifty stone masks of Chac, one group set up against the other in columns, cover the facade of the *Codz Poop* edifice at Kabah, which is 147 feet long and twenty feet high. The name *Codz Poop*, or "rolled mat," derives from an internal entrance to the structure whose access step is a long nose of Chac, curled up on itself like a mat. Chac, the god of rain, is extremely prominent here, as in many Mayan sites, despite the fact that Bishop de Landa and the codices record that the divinities of the peninsula were numerous and other gods were often as venerated as Chac. The greatest god, it is said, was Hunab Ku, creator of the world, father of all the divinities, and the

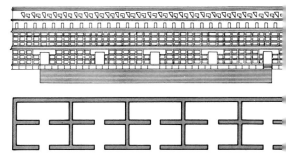

Kabah: House II. The great simplicity of this facade contrasts with the heavily decorated facade of the "Codz Poop."

god responsible for the floods that destroyed the three worlds that preceded that of the Maya. Hunab Ku was too far from men to be an object of worship, however. This was not the case with the four divine brothers, *bacab*, who survived the floods and had to hold up the sky from the four corners of the world. (The four cardinal points had colors of their own; a magic color had to correspond to its orientation.) The rain god Chac, associated with the four cardinal points and the *bacabs*, thus became Chac Xib Chac (the "Red Chac of the East") or Sac Xib Chac (the "white Chac of the North") or Ek Xib Chac, (the "Black Chac of the West"), and, lastly, Kan Xib Chac, (the "Yellow Chac of the South").

Gradually, in the Mayan culture, Chac appears to have dethroned Itzamná, the Lord of Heaven, who was the son of Hunab Ku. In the codices, Itzamná is depicted as an old toothless man with sunken cheeks and the beak of an eagle. At times he wears a beard and has one long tooth in his upper jaw. He is good and is a great friend of man. He was supposedly the inventor of writing, the codices, and the calendars. Ixchel, his wife, is the goddess of floods, of pregnant women and weaving; she also symbolizes the moon. Other gods in the Mayan world were, in order of their importance: Yum Kax, god of maize; Ah Puch, god of death; Xaman Ek, god of the polar star; and Kukulkán, the Plumed Serpent.

Sayil, Xlapak, Labná

South of Uxmal and Kabah there are many sites where explorations and restoration work have begun only recently. In this area, the Mexican School has concentrated on two centers: Sayil and Labná. On the road leading to Sayil and Labná, another site, that of Xlapak, offers visitors an image of what the ruins of Yucatán were like before the arrival of the archaeologists. It is unexcavated, and covered by vegetation.

Three outstanding monuments have emerged from the excavations at Sayil and Labná: the Palace of Sayil, the Arch of Labná, and the Palace of Labná. Partially restored, the Sayil Palace presents a completely new aspect in Mayan architecture. The edifice (276 feet by 130 feet wide) has two stories; more precisely, it is built on two levels. The upper floor is set back from the lower one and rests on a nucleus of stones and cement, which acts as a terrace. Stone columns with bordered shafts, Chac masks, and other motifs characteristic of the *Puuc* (Yucatán Maya) style alternate harmoniously with the facades of the palace.

The Arch of Labná serves as a passage between two building complexes. It is thirteen feet long and ten feet deep and is flanked by two small halls whose entranceways open onto the principal facade looking northeast. Sharply protruding cornices frame a mosaic frieze that is reminiscent of Uxmal. Two huts of carved stone, as wide as the doors they surmount, are crowned by other roofs where straw gives way to rows of feather decorations. Greek-style fluting, with a background of small columns, decorates the rear facade.

No overall plan seems to govern the Palace of Labná. The *Puuc* style of the facade is of a new type. Alternating small columns and vertical panels decorate the lower portion, whose bas-reliefs represent an interlacing of mats. This is a highly decorative motif, a symbol of command, and the beginning of the solar year. On the upper part of the facade, between two cornices, Chac masks alternate with Greek-style fluting and groups of three small columns.

An extraordinary mask of Chac, the only one of its kind in the Yucatán, is attached to the corner of the palace. The stone jaws open up like the mouth of a serpent which is about to spit out a human head — a head that could belong to an adolescent; the nose, in the form of an elephant trunk, rolls up toward the forehead, and feathers decorate the eyes. The subject of a serpent vomiting a human is typical of Mayan art. At Labná it is perhaps not a divinity emerging from the jaws of a serpent, but rather an anthropomorphic representation of the god itself.

Soil and Agriculture

Peasants, descendants of the Mayas who built these centers, live today in the surrounding areas of Labná and Sayil. These men of the twentieth century still cultivate maize with the archaic techniques of the past. Every year, armed with long planting implements, they dig into the stony land and plant the grains of maize that will give them a harvest barely necessary for survival. The cultivation of maize, the basis of their diet, governs most of their daily activities. On fixed dates they deforest, burn, plant, harvest, and then begin the same cycle over again. Despite this rotation system, however, the terrain is quickly exhausted.

Primitive agriculture is not the only factor responsible for the gradual destruction of this land. An important role in the past was played by the building of the Mayan cities, which required millions of tons of cement — which was in turn prepared by the burning of wood. In

Sayil: The Palace. This large building (276 x 130 feet) has two floors, one set back from the other. The "Puuc" style of the facade is evident in its stone columns with bordered shafts, the Chac masks, and the small decorative columns.

Sayil: The Palace. Detail from the first floor facade. The imposing mask of Chac reveals a prominent row of fangs that stress the absence of jaws. The mask crowns a series of small stone columns that are reminiscent of the wooden pillars of the Mayan huts.

Sayil: The Palace. Schematic drawing and plan. The edifice originally consisted of fifty rooms set in double rows.

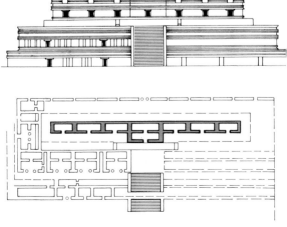

A PROPHECY FOR KATUN 11 AHAU

The fulfillment of its prophecy is ascribed to the east. The katun is establishment at Ichcaanzihoo.

This is a record of the things which they did. After it had all passed, they told of it in their own words, but its meaning is not plain. Still the course of events was as it is written. But even when everything shall be thoroughly explained, perhaps not so much is written about it, nor has very much been written of the guilt of their conspiracies with one another. So it was with the ruler of the Itzá, with the men who were rulers of Izamal, Ake, Uxmal, Ichcanziho and Citab Couoh also. Very many were the head-chiefs and many a conspiracy they made with one another. But they are not made known in what is written here; not so much will be related. Still he who comes of our lineage will know it, one of us who are Maya men. He will know how to explain these things when he reads what is here. When he sees it, then he will explain the adjustment of the intricacy of the katun by our priest, Ah Kin Xuluc; but Xuluc was not his name formerly. It was only because these priests of ours were to come to an end when misery was introduced, when Christianity was introduced by the real Christians. Then with the true God, the true Dios, came the beginning of our misery. It was the beginning of tribute, the beginning of church dues, the beginning of strife with purse-snatching, the beginning of strife with blow-guns, the beginning of strife by trampling on people, the beginning of robbery with violence, the beginning of forced debts, the beginning of debts enforced by false testimony, the beginning of individual strife, a beginning of vexation, a beginning of robbery with violence. This was the origin of service to the Spaniards and priests, of service to the local chiefs, of service to the teachers, of service to the public prosecutors by the boys, the youths of the town, while the poor people were harassed. These were the very poor people who did not depart when oppression was put upon them. It was by Antichrist on earth, the kinkajous of the towns, the foxes of the towns, the blood-sucking insects of the town, those who drained the poverty of the working people. But it shall still come to pass that tears shall come to the eyes of our Lord God. The justice of our Lord God shall descend upon every part of the world, straight from God upon Ah Kantenal, Ix Pucyola, the avaricious hagglers of the world.

The Book of Chilam Balam of Chumayel
(*pp. 78–79*)

Xlapak: "Puuc" style columns of the facade of a construction that has yet to be investigated completely.

order to obtain the lime needed for the cement (Mayan cement was made up of lime and marl), the Mayan furnaces consumed thousands of cubic feet of timber, which was never replaced. The furnace itself, which consisted of a circular heap of branches laid out in the form of a star, could reach a diameter of eighteen feet and a height of almost five feet. A layer of crushed calcareous stones was placed on top of this, and a great heap of branches was ignited. In the center, a modest chimney drew the smoke away on a level with the ground. The success of the operation depended on this removal of the smoke. The stones had to be burned with a slow, diffuse fire for twenty-four hours, after which they were sprinkled with water to transform them into lime.

Labná: The Arch. Schematic drawing of the eastern facade and plan of the arch.

The Calendar

Another legacy of pre-Columbian times was the magical Mayan calendar — a calendar that is still used by the Mayan Indians in Guatemala. The dates of magical years were inscribed on the stones of the first buildings of the classical cities in Petén, and they can also be found on the pages of the Mayan codices, where they served as a basis for divination.

Labná: The Arch. Large fretwork set on a backdrop of little stone columns decorate the eastern facade. A small "roof comb" crowns the structure.

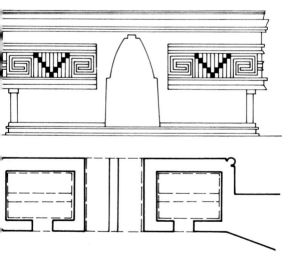

On the following pages:
Labná: The Arch. A tall corbel vault (thirteen feet wide and ten feet deep) marks the passageway between two complexes of structures. Two stylized huts are set in stone mosaic background; below them on both sides of the arch, two small rooms are oriented northeast.

Thirteen months of twenty days each — 260 days — make up the magical calendar of the Maya. The general use of a system of numbering by twenties explains the choice of the number twenty. *Uinal* in the Mayan language means twenty and has the same root as *uinic*, or man, a term which also indicates the supreme leader, *Halach uinic*. The number twenty, moreover, originated with the ten fingers of the hand and the ten toes of the foot — which seems to confirm the theory that the number twenty represented man in the magical calendars.

The presence of the number thirteen in the calendar is more ambiguous, however. This number is of great importance in Mayan civilization. According to Mayan beliefs, the celestial vault numbered thirteen heavens; thus the magical calendar could be a symbolic representation of the alliance between man and heaven.

In the magical calendar, each day of the twenty-day month had a name of its own, and each series of twenty days followed one another without intervals. And although each day was preceded by a number, these numbers did not run from one to twenty, but from one to thirteen. When the series of thirteen came to an end, the counting began from one again; these series of thirteen ciphers followed one another, parallel with the series of days, and a period of 260 was required for the calculation of the ciphers and the days to return to the starting point (1 *Imix*).

Time thus unfolded in a form composed of 260 days, at times beneficial, at times harmful, on and on into infinity. In addition to the magical values, the twenty names of days possessed a "character" of their own. Even today, in the plateaus of Guatemala, children receive the name of the day on which they are born, and supposedly take on the character of that day. In Guatemala *Imix* symbolizes the hidden forces of the universe that reveal themselves in madness; a child born on the day 1 *Imix* will bear this name, therefore, and will be considered an abnormal person whose actions are unpredictable. (The number accompanying the name possesses a particular magical value as well, which becomes part of the character of its bearer.)

In addition to the magical calendar, the Maya also adopted a solar calendar of 365 days, called *Haah*. It was made up of eighteen months of twenty days each, and one additional month of five days: *Uayeb*, or "the nameless one." Each month had a name of its own and the numbers from zero to nineteen inclusive indicated the days. The first month of the solar year was *Pop*. The solar year, therefore, began with

Labná: The Palace. The lower part of the facade is decorated in the "Puuc" style, but the geometric motifs are new characteristics.

Labná: The Palace. The lower part of the facade is decorated in the "Puuc" style, but the geometric motifs are new characteristics.

CHRISTIANITY COMES TO YUCATÁN

The face of the sun shall be turned from its course, it shall be turned face down during the reign of the perishable men, the perishable rulers. Five days the sun is eclipsed, and then shall be seen the torch of Katun 13 Ahau, a sign given by God that death shall come to the rulers of this land. Thus it shall come about that the first rulers are driven from their towns. Then Christianity shall have come here to the land.

Thus it is that God, our Father, gives a sign when they shall come, because there is no agreement. The descendants of the former rulers are dishonored and brought to misery; we are christianized, while they treat us like animals. There is sorrow in the heart of God because of these fruit-suckers.

In the year Fifteen hundred and thirty-nine, 1539, to the east was the door of the House of Don Juan Montejo, to introduce Christianity here to the land of Yucalpeten, Yucatán.

The Book of Chilam Balam of Chumayel
(p. 112)

BUILDING THE MOUNDS

The history which I have written of how the mounds came to be constructed by the heathen. During three score and fifteen katuns they were constructed. The great men made them. Then the remainder of the men went to Cartabona, as the land where they were is called today. There they were when San Bernabé came to teach them. Then they were killed by the men; the men were called heathen. 1,556 is the total count today after fifteen years. On this day I have written how the great mounds came to be built by the lineages and all the things which the rulers did. They were the ones who built the mounds. It took thirteen katuns and six years for them to construct them. The following was the beginning of the mounds they built. Fifteen four-hundreds were the scores of their mounds, and fifty more made the total count of the mounds they constructed all over the land. From the sea to the base of the land they created names for them as well as for the wells. Then a miracle was performed for them by God. Then they were burned by fire among the people of Israel. This is the record of the katuns and years since Chac-unezcab of the lineage of the Tutul Xius departed from Viroa.

The Book of Chilam Balam of Chumayel
(pp. 79–80)

the date "0 *Pop*" and the first month ended with "19 *Pop*." The last day of the year was *Uayeb* 4.

According to the Mayas, the number thirteen was joined to twenty to control the life of man from birth on. For life to unfold in a normal fashion, it was necessary to join the magical and solar calendars. Thus, the first day of the magical calendar, 1 *Imix*, began at the same time as the first day of the solar calendar, 0 *Pop*. It then took a period of fifty-two years before these two days coincided again. Specialists often represent this relationship between magical and solar time by the meshing of two cogwheels. In order to return to the starting point, the small wheel must revolve seventy-three times, which is equivalent to seventy-three years, and the large one fifty-two. This explains the origin of the well-known cycle of fifty-two years that governed the life of the Aztecs; they had borrowed the cycle from the Maya.

The Maya apparently felt that the expiration of the cycle could bring the end of the world: at that fateful moment, however, human sacrifices and a collective supplication could be made so that the gods might authorize one more life cycle. With the Maya, this cyclic time was divided between the four corners of the horizon, where the column of thirteen superimposed years loomed.

The Short Count

In order to calculate time from a chronological starting point, which has been ascertained as 3113 B.C., the Maya used a system of twentieth positions with a vertical progression. The *katun*, a period of twenty years containing 360 days each, gave this scale of twenty units a rhythm. At the end of each *katun*, the Maya erected stelae. Every 360-day year ended on the magical calendar with the day *Ahau*, the last of the series of twenty magical days. Because both calendars were based on the number twenty, the end of every *katun* always fell on *Ahau* day. But the numbers that preceded it were not the same. The Maya observed that such ciphers differed by two units at the end of every *katun*, for thirteen consecutive times, before returning to the starting cipher. Thus, when one *katun* ended the 13 *Ahau*, the next ended 11 *Ahau*, the next 9 *Ahau*, and so on. On Stele E in Quiriguá it says: 9 *baktun*, 17 *katun*, 0 *tun*, 0 *Uninal*, 0 *kin*, 13 *Ahau*, 18 *Cumbu*; from the chronological starting point, therefore, 9 periods of 144,000 days have gone by, 17 of 7,200, 0 of 360, 0 of twenty, 0 of 1 day. The name of the magical calendar day falling at the end of *katun* 17 was *Ahau* 13, while the erection of Stele E took place on the eighteenth day of the month *Cumbu*.

Around the eighth century, the Maya of the south often expressed dates with only three glyphs — a system called "end-of-period dating." With this system, the date of Stele E in Quiriguá would be expressed as follows: *Katun* 17, *Ahau* 13, *Cumbu* 18. This was sufficient for the exact notation of a date in a cycle of 19,000 years. Later in the Yucatán, however, this simplification became still more radical. Only the day *Ahau* was expressed, accompanied by the relative cipher. This was the so-called Short Count, which came into use around the eleventh century. For example, the inscription *Ahau* 13 would have been enough for the Maya of the Yucatán to express the date of Stele E in Quiriguá. This extreme simplification enabled them to annotate dates in a cycle of only 260 years, and with a margin of error of at least ten years. The *Books of Chilam Balam* use the Short Count, rather than the previous, more complex Long Count, and the chronology established through the books is subject to errors.

THE FIRST SETTLEMENTS

"Truly we endured many hardships when we came to settle in our towns," our grandfathers said of old, oh, my sons! They had brought nothing to eat, to nourish the stomach. Nor did they have anything with which to clothe themselves. Everything was lacking. We lived only on the sap of plants, we smelled the ends of our staffs to satisfy our stomachs.

It was then that we began to sow our corn. We cut down the trees, we burned them, and we sowed the seed. Thus we secured a little nourishment. Thus also we made our clothes; beating the bark of the trees and the maguey leaves, we made our clothing. As soon as we had a little corn, the buzzards appeared in the sky and swooped down over the corn field, eating a part of our food. This the people of long ago related.

The Annals of the Cakchiquels
(pp. 81–82)

THE DEATH OF THE KINGS

These kings and forefathers of ours, Oxlahuh Tzíi and Lahuh Ah, were truly feared because of their courage. They were feared also because of their wisdom, for they had not forgotten the lessons of their fathers and grandfathers. Therefore the hearts of the vassals were filled with satisfaction when those two began to rule, surrounded with glory and majesty. They had to fight many great wars. Afterwards King Cablahuh Tihax, as he was called, eldest son of King Lahuh Ah, began to govern. King Oxlahuh Tzíi also reigned while Cablahuh Tihax was ruling, and these kings likewise enjoyed great power.

Then King Qikab died, the prodigious king of the Quiché, and the Quichés began to make war on the Cakchiquels. At that time the kings called Tepepul and Iztayul ruled among the Quiché, and the Quichés hated the city of Yximché.

A great famine occurred at that time, caused by heavy frosts which killed the corn crops in the month of Uchum. The frost destroyed the plantations and the crops were lost, so our forefathers related, oh, my sons! During those days the Quichés captured a man who had escaped from the Cakchiquels and came before the Quichés bringing the news of the famine. That man spoke to them thus: "The famine is truly terrible and the people can not endure more because of the famine." Thus he said when he came before the Quichés, and these people at once determined upon the death of the Cakchiquels because they had a mortal hatred for them.

The Annals of the Cakchiquels
(pp. 10–1102)

Labná: The Palace. A group of three columns decorates the lower corner of the facade. In the upper part, this version of a Chac mask has wide-open jaws.

THE DEMAND FOR MONEY

Then Tunatiuh asked the kings for money. He wished them to give him piles of metal, their vessels and crowns. And as they did not bring them to him immediately, Tunatiuh became angry with the kings and said to them: "Why have you not brought me the metal? If you do not bring with you all of the money of the tribes, I will burn you and I will hang you," he said to the lords.

Next Tunatiuh ordered them to pay twelve hundred pesos of gold. The kings tried to have the amount reduced and they began to weep, but Tunatiuh did not consent, and he said to them: "Get the metal and bring it within five days. Woe to you if you do not bring it! I know my heart!" Thus he said to the lords.

They had already delivered half of the money to Tunatiuh when a man, an agent of the devil, appeared and said to the kings: "I am the lightning. I will kill the Spaniards; by the fire they shall perish. When I strike the drum, depart everyone from the city, let the lords go to the other side of the river. This I will do on the day 7 Ahmak August 26, 1524." Thus that demon spoke to the lords. And indeed the lords believed that they should obey the orders of that man. Half of the money had already been delivered when we escaped.

The Annals of the Cakchiquels
(pp. 123–24)

DESTRUCTION OF THE QUICHÉ MAYA

When the sun rose on the horizon and shed its light over the mountain, the war cries broke out and the banners were unfurled; the great flutes, the drums, and the shells resounded. It was truly terrible when the Quichés arrived. They advanced rapidly, and their ranks could be seen at once descending to the foot of the mountain. They soon reached the bank of the river, cutting off the river houses. They were followed by the kings Tepepul and Iztayul, who accompanied the god. Then came the encounter. The clash was truly terrible. The shouts rang out, the war cries, the sound of flutes, the beating of drums and the shells, while the warriors performed their feats of magic. Soon the Quichés were defeated, they ceased to fight and were routed, annihilated, and killed. It was impossible to count the dead.

As a result, they were conquered and made prisoner, and the kings Tepepul and Iztayul surrendered and delivered up their god. In this manner the Galel Achih the Ahpop Achí, the grandson and the son of the king, the Ahxit, the Ahpuvak, the Ahtzib, and the Ahqot, and all the warriors were annihilated and executed. The Quichés whom the Cakchiquels killed on that occasion could not be estimated at eight thousand nor at sixteen thousand. Thus our fathers and grandfathers related, oh, my sons! This is what they did, the kings Oxlahuh Tzii and Cablahuh Tihax, together with Voo Ymox and Rokel Batzín. And not otherwise did the place of Yximché become great.

The Annals of the Cakchiquels
(pp. 103–104)

Labná: The Palace. Detail from the facade. The stone jaws of the Chac mask open to spew forth a human head, while the trunk nose rolls toward the forehead.

Tulúm

When Francisco Hernandez de Cordoba and his men arrived on the coast of Mexico in March, 1517, they were met by four long canoes carrying thirty Indians. The cotton tunics and girdles of the Indians astonished the Spaniards. One of their chronicles reads: "These wild men are more reasonable than the Indians of Cuba who go completely naked."

The intentions of the Indians appeared to be friendly, but as soon as the Spaniards landed, the Indians attacked with lance thrusts and a volley of arrows, using round wooden shields and cotton "armor" to protect themselves. They could not stand up against the Spanish gunfire very long, however, and in the end they fled, leaving fifteen dead and two prisoners.

The Spaniards' two prisoners were so cross-eyed that the victors were bewildered; they did not know that this was a custom of the Maya. By hanging a small ball of resin tied with a lock of hair between the eyebrows of young children, and gluing a sphere decorated with red feathers on their foreheads, the parents rendered their children cross-eyed for the rest of their lives — and, to their taste, more esthetically pleasing. This practice explains the peculiar shape of the eyes of certain personages carved into Mayan stelae. Another custom was to flatten the forehead from infancy by placing a small board on the forehead pressing inward. This flattening can also be distinguished in the Mayan personages on the bas-reliefs.

The city that the Spaniards entered when they pursued the coastal Indians was Tulúm, today an archaeological site on the coasts of Quintana Roo, facing the island of Cozumel. Tulúm stands above a limestone cliff forty feet high, and is sheltered by a wall of stone twelve feet high and nine feet thick; this wall was a relatively important defense for the Indians, since it extended for 2,200 feet. Five narrow entrances pierced the wall. This is the second city-fortress in the Mayan lands of the Yucatán. Like the other, Mayapán, Tulúm was deeply marked by the Toltec imprint. The primitive name of the city was *Zama* (city of dawn); in the Mayan language Tulúm means "fortress."

Despite the isolation of Tulúm, traces of an ancient road have been found between Chichén-Itzá and Tulúm passing through Cobá. The road was supposedly built for religious reasons, as Tulúm was the point of embarkation for the many pilgrims who went to the island of Cozumel to worship the goddess Ixchel. After Chichén-Itzá and its Cenote of the Sacrifices, Cozumel apparently occupied second place among the pilgrimage centers of the Yucatán. Tulúm, for its part, was distinguished by its veneration of a heretofore unknown divinity. In most of the vertical niches carved above the entrance to the buildings, statues of a "descending god" have been found, a divinity about which nothing is known: neither his name, his functions, nor his powers. This stucco idol is represented with his head down and his legs in the air, spread wide apart. He has the tail of a bird, and wings are fixed to his arms and his shoulders. His hands are joined and he wears a crown on his head.

No other such representation has been found in classical Mayan art. The idol does appear, in the Mayan codices, assimilated with Itzamná, but Itzamná appears in the stucco molding on the corners of the buildings in Tulúm, bearing no resemblance to his neighbor, the descending god. One authority has singled out in the Mexican codices a god that dives downward, thus impersonating the setting of the sun; the fact that Tulúm was at first called "the city of dawn" does seem to conform with this identification.

SONG ON THE MOUNTAIN

There were their mountains and their valleys, whence had come Balam-Quitzé, Balam-Acab, Mahucutah, and Iqui-Balam, as they were called.

But it was here where they multiplied, on the mountain, and this was their town; here they were, too, when the sun, the moon, and the stars appeared, when it dawned and the face of the earth and the whole world was lighted. Here, too, began their song, which they call camucú, they sang it, but only the pain in their hearts and their innermost selves they expressed in their song. "Oh pity us! In Tulán we were lost, we were separated, and there our older and younger brothers stayed. Ah, we have seen the sun! but where are they now, that it has dawned?" so said the priests and the sacrificers of the Yaqui.

POPOL VUH
(pp. 188–89)

VICTORY OF THE BEES

They were there, then, Balam-Quitzé, Balam-Acab, Mahucutah, and Iqui-Balam, were all together on the mountain with their wives and their children when all the warriors and soldiers came. The tribes did not number sixteen thousand, or twenty-four thousand men, but even more.

They surrounded the town, crying out loudly, armed with arrows and shields, beating drums, giving war whoops, whistling, shouting, inciting them to fight, when they arrived in front of the town.

But the priests and sacrificers were not frightened; they only looked at them from the edge of the wall, where they were in good order with their wives and children. They thought only of the strength and the shouting of the tribes when they came up the side of the mountain.

Shortly before they were about to throw themselves at the entrance of the town, the four gourds which were at the edge of the town were opened and the bumblebees and the wasps came out of the gourds; like a great cloud of smoke they emerged from the gourds. And thus the warriors perished because of the insects which stung the pupils of their eyes, and fastened themselves to their noses, their mouths, their legs, and their arms. "Where are they," they said, "those who went to get and bring in all the bumblebees and wasps that are here?"

They went straight to sting the pupils of their eyes, the little insects buzzing in swarms over each one of the men; and the latter, stunned by the bumblebees and wasps, could no longer grasp their bows and their shields, which were broken on the ground.

POPOL VUH
(pp. 202–203)

Architecture and Frescoes

Most of the buildings within the walls of Tulúm share a unique architectural characteristic: the walls are slightly flared upward, both to obtain the effect of perspective and to create areas of shadow that highlight the sculptured relief. But the objective of the builders might also have been of a purely functional nature: to facilitate the draining of rain water to avoid damaging the painted stucco molding set into the corners of the buildings.

Perhaps the only building at Tulúm worthy of extended description is the most imposing: the "Castillo." This great temple rises up near the sea, prolonging the rocky part of the shore in such a way that it appears to be a full-scale fortress. It is made up of three terraced stories, each of which bears a small sanctuary. The monumental aspect of the "Castillo" is accentuated by a broad central stairway that rises to the top terrace and leads to the main sanctuary. This latter structure, of modest dimensions, consists of two small vaulted halls. Two pillars in the form of serpents support the portico. Three rectangular niches fit into the molding of the frieze, the center one containing the statue of the descending god.

Inside the "Castillo," Temple V, and the Temple of the Frescoes, several series of murals are still relatively well preserved. These paintings are not in the Mayan style, and a relationship has been established between these frescoes and those of Santa Rita, in British Honduras,

Tulúm: The Castillo. The city rises from the top of a forty-foot cliff over the Caribbean Sea on the coast of Quintana Roo, opposite the island of Cozumel. This was the first Mexican city to be discovered by the Spanish in 1517.

Tulúm: The Castillo. The back of the large temple faces the sea. A large central stairway rising to the top terrace accentuates the monumental aspect of this structure. Two pillars in the form of serpents support the portico. Three rectangular niches interrupt the molding of the frieze.

INTERROGATION OF THE CHIEFS

These are the words. If they are not understood by the chiefs of the towns, ill-omened is the star adorning the night. Frightful is its house. Sad is the havoc in the courtyards of the nobles. Those who die are those who do not understand; those who live will understand it. This competitive test shall hang over the chiefs of the towns; it has been copied so that the severity may be known in which the reign is to end. Their hands are bound before them to a wooden collar. They are pulled along with the cord. They are taken to the house of the ruler, the first head-chief. This is the end of the chiefs. This shall hang over the unrestrained lewd ones of the day and of the katun. They shall feel anguish when the affairs of the chiefs of the towns shall come to an end. This shall occur on the day when the law of the katun shall come to an end, when Katun 3 Ahau shall terminate. The chiefs of the towns shall be seized because they are lacking in understanding.

The Book of Chilam Balam of Chumayel
(pp. 91–92)

Tulúm: The Castillo. Vertical view and schematic drawing showing successive constructions.

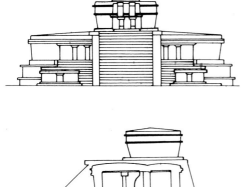

which are themselves supposedly related to the murals of Milta on the central plateau of Mexico. Nevertheless, the subjects represented in the Tulúm murals are essentially Mayan — such as the personage with the long nose and the scepters in the form of little men.

Here and there impressions of red hands mark the walls of Temple V. These are oddly reminiscent of those left by prehistoric men on the walls of their caves. In Mexico, the Aztec god Macuilxochitl, "five flowers," who patronized music and dance, was always painted red; a white hand — symbol of the number five which enters into the composition of his name — surrounded his mouth. Perhaps the hand-prints on the walls of the Temple V are signs that the figures belong to a dance group, and possibly the sanctuary was a place reserved for sacred dancers. Also, in the magical events outlined in the legendary tales of the migration of Quetzalcoatl, mention is made of the spontaneous apparition of handprints wherever he passed. It could be, then, that the handprints on the walls of the Tulúm temple symbolize the passage of Quetzalcoatl; or perhaps they are a sign of the reign of the Toltecs in this city.

Despite the Toltec-inspired nature of some of these monuments, Tulúm's Stele I appears to indicate an authentically classical Mayan origin of the site. Its hieroglyphic inscriptions, the date of which has been deciphered, says: 9.6.10.0.0.8. *Ahau* 13 Pax, or January 29, A.D. 654. Stele II bears the inscription: *katun* 2 *Ahau.* (1263), which is a date of the Short Count. Stele I, which appears to be proof of the message brought to these regions by the Mayan emigrants of Petén, carries an "initial series" date indicating that there was a vast cultural context for it. Stele II, with the extreme simplification of its date, brings to mind the later reign of the warriors from the north.

THE EXECUTION OF TOLGOM

Then began the execution of Tolgom. He dressed and covered himself with his ornaments. Then they tied him with his arms extended to a poplar tree to shoot him with arrows. Afterwards all the warriors began to dance. The music to which they danced is called the song of Tolgom. Following this they began to shoot the arrows, but no one of them hit the cords with which he was tied, but instead they fell beyond the gourd tree, in the place of Qakbatzulú where all the arrows fell. At last our ancestor Gagavitz shot the arrow which flew directly to the spot called Cheetzulú and pierced Tolgom. After which all of the warriors killed him. Some of the arrows entered his body and others fell farther away. And when that man died, his blood was shed in abundance behind the poplar. Then they came and completed the division of pieces of him among all the warriors of the seven tribes that took part in the offering and the sacrifice, and his death was commemorated thereafter in the month of Uchum. Every year they gathered for their festivals and orgies and shot at the children, but instead of arrows they shot at them with alder branches as though they were Tolgom. Thus our grandfathers related of old, oh, our sons!

In this manner we the Zotzils and Tukuchés together gained knowledge of magic science and of greatness and power. All humbled themselves before the fathers and grandfathers of us the Cakchiquels; and the glory of the birth of our early fathers was never extinguished.

The Annals of the Cakchiquels
(*pp. 74–75*)

Dzibilchaltún

Dzibilchaltún, "the place where there are symbols inscribed on flat stones," is a Mayan archaeological site in the Yucatán some ten miles north of Mérida. There is no trace of this settlement in the Spanish chronicles, although the scholar A. Barrera-Vasquez believes that in the sixteenth century it was called Holtun Chable. In any case, the indigenous religious center on this site was razed by the Spaniards so that they could build a Catholic church with the stones of the demolished temples.

Until 1956, practically all that was known of Dzibilchaltún was its bizarre name. In reality, it is one of the most extensive complexes of pre-Columbian ruins. It covers a surface of thirty square miles, and presents a quantity of buildings found in no other archaeological site in the Yucatán.

During a preliminary investigation of this site in 1941, two American archaeologists, George W. Brainerd and E. Wyllys Andrews, stressed the importance of Dzibilchaltún and noted that it had very ancient origins. Nevertheless, the entire western section of the city continued to be plundered and destroyed by local building entrepreneurs. Finally in 1956 an important excavation was begun under the direction of Andrews. When divers explored the cenote of Xlacah, at the center of the site, some 30,000 objects of archaeological interest were found at a depth of 146 feet. Although this seemed to prove that the locality was once a site of pilgrimages, perhaps as well known as Chichén-Itzá, no theories were proposed until the end of the excavations in 1961.

When the excavation reports were made available to scholars, the news quickly spread that the data collected at Dzibilchaltún were highly significant. Through architectural details and ceramics, experts determined that the city's settlement extended without interruption from the pre-classical Mayan age (from about 600 B.C.) to a date considerably later than the Spanish colonization of the Yucatán. This indicated that the priority of the occupation of the Petén region, compared to that of Yucatán, was a concept to be reconsidered. It was in fact likely that the Mayan sites in the Yucatán were just as old as the cities of the south and that they were perhaps wholly independent, not colonies.

In a word, the excavations at Dzibilchaltún do apparently prove that the Mayan civilization developed on parallel lines in both north and south. As far back as 1962 the Mexican specialist Marta Foncerrada de Molina wrote: "Mayan sources speak of the arrival of populations, of the founding and abandoning of the cities, of internal difficulties, and even of personal conflicts. This (information) must serve investigators solely as a point of reference, as weak allusions to certain sites and to the presence of cultural elements extraneous to an autochthonous tradition. But the written source, in this specific case, will not clarify historical reality if this is not confirmed by archaeological elements and by a stylistic study of the monuments. It is known that in the world that preceded the Spanish Conquest, history was frequently rewritten, and that facts and dates were adapted to the cultural model of the people setting it down." (*Estudios de Cultura Maya*, Vol. II, p. 137, Mexico City, 1962.)

If the discoveries of Dzibilchaltún do justify this extreme position, then the site, at least for the present, remains the only one of its kind. And this new discovery, after all, does not necessarily push the origins of previously known centers in the Yucatán further into the past. The historical chronicles, even the rather subjective, partial, erroneous ones, tend to confirm the data supplied by several of the "initial series" dates in the hieroglyphic inscriptions at various sites. The abundance of "initial series" dates in the classical centers of Petén, as compared to their rarity in the Yucatán peninsula, tends to confirm the cultural

Dzibilchaltún: Temple of the Seven Dolls, officially known as Structure I sub. The two windows in the sides of the main entranceway, the square plan, and the pyramid form of the roof comb are unique in Mayan architecture.

Dzibilchaltún: Temple of the Seven Dolls. Plan and schematic drawing with the two windows and the roof comb in the form of a truncated pyramid.

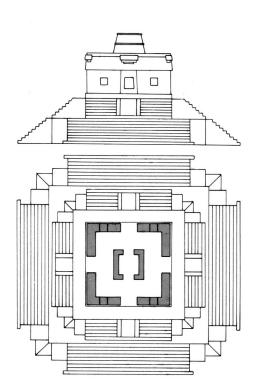

priority of the Maya of the classical period in the Petén region and other areas to the south. The theory that depicts the south as the cradle of the Mayan culture, then, can at least maintain its credibility until further research is completed. Meanwhile, the disclosures from Dzibilchaltún should make everyone wary of hasty generalizations.

Stele 9 and the Temple of the Seven Dolls

Although in a poor state of conservation, the hieroglyphic inscription on Stele 9 at Dzibilchaltún has been successfully deciphered. The initial series reads: 8.14.10.0.0., which converts to the year A.D. 327, one of the oldest dates known to be inscribed on a stele, either in the Yucatán or in Petén. Indeed, there are only two dates known to be older. One is on the jade Leyden Plaque, found near Puerto Barrios, Guatemala but sculptured in the Tikal style; it bears the date that converts to A.D. 320. And the oldest of all known dates is that of Stele 29 at Tikal, whose initial series reads 8.12.14.8.15 — A.D. 292.

Another indication of Dzibilchaltún's age is the Temple of the Seven Dolls (technically known as Structure 1 sub), which has been dated as a fifth century structure by carbon-14 analysis. It is to this exceptional edifice, in part at least, that Dzibilchaltún owes its fame. The temple is unusual because of its square plan, which is unique in Mayan architecture, and also because of its windows, placed on either side of the main entrance. No other Mayan edifice has had windows — a phenomenon that cannot be explained as a "late" innovation because of the temple's age.

The temple takes its informal name from the seven statues of monstrous personages that it contains. The roof comb of the structure is also unusual. While the roof comb on most Mayan structures gives lightness and balance to their heavy bases, the one on this temple forms a truncated pyramid. Indications are that it is a primitive decoration, erected in an attempt to adapt the corbel vault to the square plan of the temple.

SOME KATUN PROPHECIES

Katun 10 Ahau, the katun is established at Chable. The ladder is set up over the rulers of the land. The hoof shall burn; the sand by the seashore shall burn; the bird's nest shall burn. The rocks shall crack with the heat; drought is the charge of the katun. It is the word of our Lord God the Father and of the Mistress of Heaven, the portent of the katun. No one shall arrest the word of our Lord God, God the Son, the Lord of Heaven and earth. There shall not be lacking that which shall, through his power, come to pass all over the world. Holy Christianity shall come bringing with it the time when the stupid ones who speak our language badly shall turn from their evil ways. No one shall prevent it; this then is the drought. Sufficient is the word for the Maya priests, the word of God.

Katun 8 Ahau is the ninth katun. The katun is established at Izamal. There is Kinich Kakmo, The shield shall descend, the arrow shall descend upon Chakanputun together with the rulers of the land. The heads of the foreigners to the land were cemented into the wall at Chakanputun. There is an end of greed; there is an end to causing vexation in the world. It is the word of God the Father. Much fighting shall be done by the natives of the land.

Katun 4 Ahau is the eleventh katun according to the count. The katun is established at Chichén-Itzá. The settlement of the Itzá shall take place there. The quetzal shall come, the green bird shall come. Ah Kantenal shall come. Blood-vomit shall come. Kukulcan shall come with them for the second time. It is the word of God. The Itzá shall come.

Katun 2 Ahau is the twelfth katun. At Maya [uaz] Cuzamil the katun is established. For half the katun there will be bread; for half the katun there will be water. It is the word of God. For half of it there will be a temple for the rulers. It is the end of the word of God.

Behold, when they come, there is no truth in the words of the foreigners to the land. They tell very solemn and mysterious things, the sons of the men of Seven-deserted-buildings, the offspring of the women of Seven-deserted-buildings, lord.

Who will be the prophet, who will be the priest who shall interpret truly the word of the book?

The Book of Chilam Balam of Chumayel
(pp. 159–169)

APPENDICES
THE MONUMENTS THROUGH THE AGES

Chronicles

A study of the many books written about the Mayan world reveals the diversity of this civilization, and at times its outright contradictions. As far back as the first sixteenth-century manuscripts the narrators fall into several categories. First, there were the adventurers, such as *Juan Diaz, Pedro Martyr,* and *Bernal Diaz del Castillo,* whose accounts are full of discovery, wonder, and admiration. Our modern interest in these documents lies in the importance of the discoveries they describe. Castillo, in particular, offers a narrative of acute details, excellent descriptions of the monuments, and useful observations on the populations he encountered. The chronicles of the Spanish leaders also date from this period — those of *Cortés* and his lieutenants, *Alvarado,* the conqueror of Guatemala, and the *Monteyos,* father and son, who conquered the Yucatán. But these accounts are limited, and ultimately stress the tactical abilities of the leaders themselves rather than a description of the people they sought to conquer. These accounts seek to justify actions to military superiors, to the King of Spain, and perhaps to posterity.

The next category of writers contains the authors of memoirs and the comments of men who arrived in the Mayan lands a few years after the Conquest: *Bienvenida, Ciudad Real, Palacios,* and, above all, *Bishop Diego de Landa.* The aim of these so-called missionaries was to wipe out the last vestiges of the Indian civilization and replace it with a Christian outlook. Fortunately, these Europeans did attempt to reconstruct the past in their accounts. During this era the exceptional personality of *Bartolemé de La Casas* stands out. This Spanish monk dedicated his life to the salvation of the Indians and made every effort to convince his Spanish countrymen that the inhabitants of the new lands were in fact "human beings." He even invented a biblical origin for them, contending that they were descendants of one of the lost tribes of Israel.

Oviedo, Gomara, Herrera, Garcia, and *Torquemada,* historians at the end of the sixteenth century, wrote their works concerning the Mayas on the basis of previous documents; they did not offer firsthand information. The seventeenth century boasts of an excellent Yucatán historian, *Diego Lopez Cogulludo.* His colleague from Guatemala, *Fuentes y Guzman,* on the other hand, is known for his fantasy and imagination. The Englishman *Thomas Gage* was the first chronicler of Chiapas and Guatemala. The writings of *Avendaño* and *Villagutierre de Soto Mayor* dealt with the last groups of Indians to escape from the yoke of the Spanish influence. In the eighteenth century only a few historians concerned themselves with the Maya, but the first reports of the remains, illustrated with actual drawings, were being compiled by *Antonio Bernasconi, José Calderon,* and *Antonio Del Rio.*

The nineteenth century ushered in the century of the "discovery" of the Maya, as well as a time of error, recriminations, and varying interpretations. *Alexander von Humboldt,* for instance, was a German of great learning and curiosity about the New World, but his writings on the Maya, however serious, were too scanty in their evidence to advance the subject much. Then there were visionaries and theosophists such as *Lord Kingsborough* and *Augustus Le Plongeon,* who read into the unusual forms of this emergent culture proof of their own beliefs. In general, scholars of the nineteenth century were unable to break away from their classical training and Christian heritage, and so they inevitably tried to fit the Indians into the forms they were most familiar with. But several of the nineteenth century students of the Maya can still be quoted by serious twentieth century students, for men such as *John Lloyd Stephens, William H. Prescott,* or *Brasseur de Bourbourg,* whatever the deficiencies of the evidence, were careful and astute "reconstructers". The pictorial representations of *Désiré Charnay, Frédéric Waldeck,* and *Frederick Catherwood,* were also most helpful. And by the end of the century, *Alfred Maudslay,* the English scholar, was laying the groundwork for a truly scientific study of the ancient Maya, a study that many people have continued in the twentieth century.

What follows here, then, is a mere selection of excerpts from the many sources and accounts available. Through the eyes and words of many of the prime discoverers of the Maya, we glimpse the changing attitudes toward the Mayan culture and the cumulative effect of knowledge about the sites.

Bernal Diáz del Castillo (1517–1568): *Historia Verdadera de la conquista de Nueva España.*

On the eighth day of the month of February in the year 1517 we left Havana from the port of Axaruca, on the northern side, and in twelve days we doubled the point of San Antonio, which in Cuba is called Land of the Guanahataveyes (who are savage Indians). Having left this point behind and having reached the open sea, we navigated without destination toward the setting sun, knowing nothing of the winds and currents that prevailed in that latitude, at great risk to our own lives. In fact, it was at that time that we were caught by a storm that lasted two days and two nights, and which was so violent that we nearly perished. When the calm weather returned, we continued on our way, and twenty days after our departure caught sight of land and were filled with joy, giving thanks to God for our good fortune. This land had never been discovered, and up to that time no one had had the slightest suspicion of its existence. From our vessel we could make out a large city, at a distance of about two leagues; realizing that it was a particularly large settlement and that we had seen nothing to compare with it either on the Island of Cuba or on that of La Hispaniola, we named it "Great Cairo."

Hernán Cortés: *Cartas de relación de la conquista de Mexico,* (1519)

Having completed the construction of the aforementioned armada, Your Royal Highnesses' aforesaid captain, Hernán Cortés, departed from the aforementioned island Fernandina, to continue his voyage with ten caravels and four hundred soldiers, many of them mounted, including sixteen cavalrymen. Continuing the voyage, the first land they touched was the island of Cozumel, which today is called Santa Cruz, as pointed out earlier, in the port of San Juan de Porta Latina. Disembarking, they found the village abandoned, as if it had never been inhabited at all. And the aforesaid captain, Hernán Cortés, wishing to discover the reason for that abandonment, ordered his men to leave the ships and go ashore, and they took up quarters in the village. While in the village with his men, the captain learned from three Indians that had been captured on the sea in a canoe, and who had been going to the Island of Yucatán, that the inhabitants of that Island, seeing the Spaniards arrive, had abandoned the village and gone with all their Indians into the woods, for fear of those very Spaniards, in that they knew neither the intentions nor the will of those who had come here in ships. And the aforementioned Hernán Cortés, speaking to them through an intermediary he had brought along with him, told them he would harm no one.

Bishop Diego de Landa: From *Landa's Relación de las Cosas de Yucatán,* translated and edited by Alfred M. Tozzer; Vol. 18 of the Papers of the Peabody Museum of American Archaeology and Ethnology, Harvard University (Cambridge, 1941)

There are in Yucatán many beautiful buildings, which is the most remarkable thing that has been found in the Indies. They are all of stone very well hewn, although there is no metal in this country with which they could have been worked. These buildings are very close to one another and are temples; and the reason that there are so many of them is that the people changed their dwelling places many times; and in each town they built a temple, seeing that there is an extraordinary abundance of stone lime and a certain white earth which is excellent for buildings. These buildings have not been constructed by other nations than the Indians and this is seen from the naked stone men made modest by long girdles which they called in their language *ex* as well as from other devices which the Indians wear.

While the friar, the author of this book, was in this country, they discovered in a building, which they destroyed, a great urn with three handles with silver-colored flames painted outside and enclosing the ashes of a burned body with some arm and leg bones of a marvellous size, and three fine beads of stone of the same kind which the Indians use for money. These buildings of Izamal were eleven or twelve in all, without there being any recollection of the builders, and at the request of the Indians, a monastery, which they called San Antonio, was established in one of these in 1549.

After these the most important buildings are those of Tecoh and Chichén Itzá, which will be described later.

Chichén Itzá is a very fine site, ten leagues from Izamal and eleven from Valladolid. It is said that it was ruled by three lords who were brothers who came into that country from the west, who were very devout and so they built very beautiful temples and their wives lived very chastely, and one of them died or went away, upon which the other two acted unjustly and indecently and for this they were put to death. We will describe later the decoration of the principal building and will tell about the well into which they threw living men in sacrifice, as well as other beautiful things. It is more than seven stadia deep down to the water, and more than one hundred feet broad, marvellously formed by a circular and perpendicular opening in the living rock, and the water appears green. . . .

Catholic Missionary: *Report on Indians of Guatemala* (Sixteenth Century)

If one looks closely, he will find that everything these Maya Indians did and talked about was concerned with maize-corn; indeed, they almost made a god of it. And they got — and still get — so much delight and satisfaction out of their corn fields that because of them they ignore wife and children and every other pleasure, as though their corn fields were their final goal and absolute happiness.

Fray Bartolomé de Las Casas:
Apologetica Historia Sumaria
(Sixteenth Century)

It is hereby declared, demonstrated and openly concluded, from Chapter 22 up to the end of this book, that all those peoples are natives of our Indies. . . and that they possessed their republics, their localities, their villages, and their cities, sufficiently provided with food, with nothing lacking on the political and social level. . . some had more, some had less, and many had absolutely everything that was needed, because they are all highly vivacious and frank, and of a very acute understanding.

Diego Garcia de Palacios:
Carta dirigda al Rey de España. From:
Recueil de documents et mémoires originaux sur l'histoire de possessions espagnoles dans l'Amérique (1576)

Not far away, on the road to San Pedro, one discovers in the first village of the Province of Honduras, called Copán, the ruins of the splendid buildings which demonstrate that there had once been a great city here — such [a city] as it is not likely that such crude people as the local natives could have built. It was situated on the bank of a fine river, in an open well-chosen plain. The plain is highly fertile, the climate is temperate and there is an abundance of fish and wild game.

In the midst of these ruins are trees that seem to have been planted by the hand of man, and other remarkable things. Before arriving at this point, one comes upon an extremely thick wall and an enormous stone eagle. On the chest of this is a square measuring about a fourth of a "vara" on each side and bearing a number of unknown characters.

When one draws closer, one discovers the figure of a great stone giant. The old Indians say it was a guardian of the sanctuary. A little farther on is a stone cross three palms high, its transversal arm broken. One then comes upon a number of buildings in ruins, whose stones had been cut with great art, and a statue more than four "varas" high resembling a bishop with his pontifical vestments, a well-carved mitre, and a ring on its finger. Only a short distance off is a great plaza surrounded by steps that call to mind the description that is made of the Colosseum in Rome. At some points these attain a height of eighty steps, all paved with bricks of fine stone, and beautifully carved. There are six statues: three representing men with armor in mosaic, with ribbons around their legs, and with weapons studded with ornaments. The others represent women in long dresses, wearing Roman style headdresses. The statue of the bishop holds in [its] hand a small package resembling a casket. It appears that these statues were idols, because situated in front of each one of them is a stone similar to that used for sacrifices, with a tiny gutter to carry off blood. One can still see the altars on which incense was burned. In the center of the plaza is a stone basin which, it seems, was used for baptisms, and in which common sacrifices were made.

After having traversed this plaza, one comes upon an elevated point to which one climbs by a large number of steps. This is no doubt where the religious rites and the "mitotes," or feasts, were celebrated. Indications are that it was built with the greatest care, because one finds beautifully carved stones just about everywhere here. Alongside is a tower or tall terrace commanding a view of the river. . . A large layer of the wall has crumbled, exposing the entrance to two extremely long, narrow subterranean chambers, both of which were well constructed. I was unable to discover why they were built or what their purpose may have been. A stairway with a great number of steps leads down to the river.

There are many other things to be seen, and they show that this city was once inhabited by a large civilized people rather advanced in the arts. I did everything possible to find out from the Indians who it was that had built this monument, and all I could get out of questioning their old people — since in the entire country not one of their ancient books was left, and the only one I know of is in my possession — all I was able to find out, I say, was that the buildings in question had been erected by a powerful lord that had come from the Yucatán, and that after a few years he had returned to his homeland, leaving them completely deserted. And this is what is most likely, because tradition says that the Indians of the Yucatán once conquered the Province of Ayatal, Lacandón, Verapaz, Chiquimula, and Copán. It also appears that the buildings resemble those which the first Spaniards discovered in the Yucatán, on which there were figures of bishops and armed men, as well as crosses.

Thomas Gage:
The English-American. . . or, A New Survey of the West India's
(London, 1648)

There is no town in the Indies great or small (though it be but of twenty families) which is not dedicated thus unto Our Lady or unto some saint, and the remembrance of that saint is continued in the minds not only of them that live in the town, but of all that live far and near by commercing, trading, sporting, and dancing, offering unto the saint, and bowing, kneeling, and praying before him. . . .

The chief dance used amongst them is called *toncontin*, which hath been danced before the King of Spain in the Court of Madrid by Spaniards, who have lived in the Indies, to shew unto the King somewhat of the Indians' fashions; and it was reported to have pleased the King very much. This dance is thus performed. The Indians commonly that dance it (if it be a great town) are thirty or forty, or fewer if it be a small town. They are clothed in white, both their doublets, linen drawers, and *aiates*, or towels, which on the one side hang almost to the ground. Their drawers and *aiates* are wrought with some works of silk, or with birds, or bordered with some lace. Others procure doublets and drawers and *aiates* of silk, all which are hired for that purpose. On their backs they hang long tufts of feathers of all colours, which with glue are fastened into a little frame made for the purpose and gilded on the outside; this frame with ribbons they tie about their shoulders fast that it fall not, nor slacken with the motion of their bodies. Upon their heads they wear another less tuft of feathers either in their hats, or in some gilded or painted headpiece, or helmet. In their hands also they carry a fan of feathers, and on their feet most will use feathers also bound together like short wings of birds; some wear shoes, some not. And thus from top to toe they are almost covered with curious and coloured feathers. Their music and tune to this dance is only what is made with a hollow stock of a tree, being rounded and well pared within and without, very smooth and shining, some four times thicker than our viols, with two or three long clefts on the upper side and some holes at the end which they call *tepanabaz*. On this stock (which is placed upon a stool or form in the middle of the Indians) the master of the dance beats with two sticks, covered with wool at the ends, and a pitched leather over the wool that it fall not away. With this instrument and blows upon it (which soundeth but dull and heavy, but somewhat loud) he giveth the dancers their several tunes, and changes, and signs of the motion of their bodies either straight or bowing, and giveth them warning what and when they are to sing. Thus they dance in compass and circle round about that instrument, one following another sometimes straight, sometimes turning about, sometimes turning half way, sometimes bending their bodies and with the feathers in their hands almost touching the ground, and singing the life of that their saint, or of some other. All this dancing is but a kind of walking round, which they will continue two or three whole hours together in one place, and from thence go and perform the same at another house.

Diego Lopez Cogolludo,
Historia de Yucatán (1688)

Don Bartolomé, brother of the admiral (Christopher Columbus), went ashore to greet the people and saw a canoe of remarkable proportions approaching from the west. At the sight of the ships of our Spaniards they neither attempted to flee nor prepared to defend themselves, such great fear had they of these people that were so new to them. The canoe drew within sight of the admiral, who made the Indians come aboard, along with their women and children. They revealed themselves to be modest and virtuous because, the moment the clothes that covered them were taken away they would cover themselves again, which pleased the admiral very much, as well as those who were with him. . . . These Indians were from the Kingdom of Yucatán, because to the east lay the Gulf of Guanajos, a little less than thirty leagues from the island where the admiral was (and which he named "Island of Pines," because of the many trees of this kind there). Since they had come from the west he was certain they were from the Yucatán, in that there was no other land toward which they might have sailed in all safety in such a small craft, though for a canoe it was rather large, being eight feet wide.

José Calderon and Antonio Bernasconi:
Rapporto (1784)

Accompanied by a number of inhabitants of the locality, Indians and half-breeds, I went to the ruins of the city three leagues from here, in the locality known as Casas de Piedra, or the Stone Houses. First of all I caught sight of eight houses, one of which I called the "Palace" because of its exceptional size and its architecture. Then, continuing to make my way through the blackberry bushes, I came upon a large number of houses and palaces, less sumptuous than the first ones, by passing between many hills and often climbing. I found these buildings, which were situated in all directions from the Palace, during the three days the expedition lasted and in the order I have listed them. Most of them face south of the one that may perhaps be called the royal residence. The site of these buildings is impractical, both because of the density of the forest and because of the precipices surrounding them. The city cannot have been abandoned for less than three or four centuries, because many of the houses already have trees above them that are three or four aunes thick. . . . I find no one here who can give me a clear idea of what this city was like. It is a tremendous achievement, most sumptuous, though crude, and a great beauty. Various figures are carved with great skill on the walls of these palaces, which are entirely of stone. There are many human figures clad in strange clothes and plumage, women of gigantic size with children in their arms, many shields, and a sort of coat-of-arms inscription to be found in one palace in front of the door. [There is also] the unfinished tower one sees looming up in the great Palace, from whose top one can see the fields and lagoons of this entire country.

Plutarch, it is said, reports that the ancient Romans wore crescents on their boots, thus upholding the immortality of the soul. Were those who once reigned here Romans? Or were they Spaniards that at the time of the Moorish domination ventured as far as the disembarkation port of Catasaja; or then again were they Carthaginians who, some say, once came to America? I do not know.

Report of Antonio Del Rio:
Rapporto (1786–87)

From Palenque, the last locality of the Province of Ciudad Real de Chiapas, the road ascends toward the southeast, through a chain of mountains that separates this kingdom of Guatemala from that of Yucatán and Campeche. After two leagues, one arrives at a creek named Michol, whose waters flow toward the west till they join with the great river Tulija, which channels its own to the Province of Tabasco. Once the creek has been left behind, one continues to climb, and half a league farther on one crosses a small waterway called Ototun, which runs into the preceding one. It is here one begins to catch sight of masses of ruins, which makes progress anything but easy for the next half a league, up to the point where the Houses of Stone are located. There are fourteen of these houses, more or less in ruins, but which obviously still have most of their rooms intact.

A rectangular surface three hundred aunes wide and four hundred and fifty long makes up the terrace at the foot of the highest mountain in the chain. It forms a plaza, and one discovers, situated as if in the center, the largest, most spacious house of all those that have been found. It rests on an elevated area, or hill, twenty aunes in height, and all around are the other houses, which are laid out in the following manner: five to the north, four to the south, one to the southwest and three to the east. One should not fail to observe that the remains of other houses and crumbled buildings are to be seen in every direction. Since these buildings are to be seen stretching out, primarily along the mountain running from east to west, up to a distance of three or four leagues on either side, it can be said that the total extension of this city in ruins was from seven to eight leagues in length. But its width does not correspond to such an extension, being more or less only half a league to the point where the ruins cease (in other words the Michol creek flowing at the foot of the mountain). . . . Thanks to much perseverance, I was able to do everything that was necessary, so that there is not a single sealed window or door, or partition that has not been perforated, a room, a corridor, a courtyard, a tower or a subterranean passage where an excavation of at least two or three "varas" in depth has not been carried out.

Guillermo Dupaix:
Expediciones acerca de los Antiguos Monumentos de Nueva España (1805–1808)

As for the partial installation of the people of Palenque, healthy reason does not recoil at the thought that this emigration took part from the eastern part of the earth, originating from the great Island of Atlantis. . . . It would not be difficult for me to think that such a transmigration took place before and during the cataclysm, this latter having granted the time and the means for a part of the inhabitants to flee the great imminent danger. [These] inhabitants, perhaps compelled by prevailing winds to head west, might have carried with them the seeds of the arts which sent down their roots and took hold in a favorable climate, in time flowering and bearing marvelous fruit, as can be seen in the architectural achievements and the sculpture. Proof of the great antiquity of the works of art lies in the remarkable excellence they attained, because the arts and sciences are propagated with extreme slowness (without help, it is a well-known fact that they take centuries).

Alexander von Humboldt,
Vue des Cordillères (1810)

The religious who entered Mexico and Peru in the wake of the armadas of Cortés and Pizarro revealed a natural inclination to exaggerate the analogies they thought they found between the cosmogony of the Aztecs and the dogmas of the Christian religion. Imbued with Hebrew traditions, grasping only imperfectly the language of the country and the meaning of the hieroglyphic paintings, they connected everything up with the system in which they had been trained. They were similar in this to the ancient Romans, who in the Teutonic people and the Gauls recognized only their own cult and their own divinities.

Lord Kingsborough:
Antiquities of Mexico
(London, 1848)

And here we may remark that the Mexican tradition, as far as it relates to the stratagem which the ancestors of the Tlascaltecas employed to destroy the giants, so singularly agrees with the account given by Herodotus of the manner in which the Scythians were destroyed by the Medes, who having made themselves masters of a great portion of Asia, and committing all kinds of excesses, were at last slain at a banquet to which they had been invited by the Medes, who thus recovered their lost empire, that we cannot but think it extremely probable that the descendants of the Jews in the New World, who must long have retained a recollection of the event which led to the establishment of the Median monarchy, and by placing Cyrus on the throne of Persia mainly contributed to that order of things which liberated their ancestors from the Babylonian captivity, did in progress of time, when tradition had partially faded from their memory, confound the events of sacred and profane history, and form, out of the whole, an incongruous mass. . . . We may further remark, in reference [to the above passage] that the tradition of God's having destroyed a race of giants is extremely ancient, and of Hebrew origin. The address even of the Deity to the angel Gabriel on that memorable occasion is recorded in the following passage of the Book of Enoch. . . . "But to Gabriel He said, Go, Gabriel, to the giants, to the adulterous and lying sons of fornication, and destroy the sons of the Egregori from the sons of men." Having elsewhere proved that the Mexicans were acquainted with some of the traditions of the apocryphal Book of Esdras, it is almost superfluous to add, that the contents of the Book of Enoch, and other apocryphal books, might especially have been made known to them in very early ages by the first Jewish settlers in America.

John Lloyd Stephens:
Incidents of Travel in Central America, Chiapas, and Yucatán
(New York, 1858)
Courtesy of Harper & Row, Publishers.

The impression made upon our minds by these speaking but unintelligible tablets I shall not attempt to describe. From some unaccountable cause they have never before been presented to the public. Captains Del Rio and Dupaix both refer to them, but in very few words, and neither of them has given a single drawing. Acting under a royal commission, and selected, doubtless, as fit men for the duties intrusted to them, they cannot have been ignorant or insensible of their value. It is my belief they did not give them because in both cases the artists attached to their expedition were incapable of the labour, and the steady, determined perseverance required for drawing such complicated, unintelligible, and anomalous characters. As at Copán, Mr. Catherwood divided his paper into squares; the original drawings were reduced, and the engravings corrected by himself, and I believe they are as true copies as the pencil can make: the real written records of a lost people. The Indians call this building an escuela or school, but our friends the padres called it a tribunal of justice, and these stones, they said, contained the tables of the law.

There is one important fact to be noticed. The hieroglyphics are the same as were found at Copán and Quiriguá. The intermediate country is now occupied by races of Indians speaking many different languages, and entirely unintelligible to each other; but there is room for the belief that the whole of this country was once occupied by the same race, speaking the same language, or, at least, having the same written characters. . . . There was no necessity for assigning to the ruined city an immense extent, or an antiquity coeval with that of the Egyptians or of any other ancient and known people. What we had before our eyes was grand, curious, and remarkable enough. Here were the remains of a cultivated, polished, and peculiar people, who had passed through all the stages incident to the rise and fall of nations; reached their golden age, and perished, entirely unknown. The links which connected them with the human family were severed and lost, and these were the only memorials of their footsteps upon earth. We lived in the ruined palace of their kings; we went up to their desolate temples and fallen altars; and wherever we moved we saw the evidences of their taste, their skill in arts, their wealth and power. In the midst of desolation and ruin we looked back to the past, cleared away the gloomy forest, and fancied every building perfect, with its terraces and pyramids, its sculptured and painted ornaments, grand, lofty, and imposing, and overlooking an immense inhabited plain; we called back into life the strange people who gazed at us in sadness from the walls; pictured them, in fanciful costumes and adorned with plumes of feathers, ascending the terraces of the palace and the steps leading to the temples; and often we imagined a scene of unique and gorgeous beauty and magnificence, realizing the creations of Oriental poets, the very spot which fancy would have selected for the "Happy Valley" of Rasselas. In the romance of the world's history nothing ever impressed me more forcibly than the spectacle of this once great and lovely city, overturned, desolate, and lost; discovered by accident, overgrown with trees for miles around, and without even a name to distinguish it. Apart from everything else, it was a mourning witness to the world's mutations.

William H. Prescott:
History of the Conquest of Mexico
(Philadelphia, 1877)
Courtesy of J.B. Lippincott Co.

The hieroglyphics are too few on the American buildings to authorize any decisive inference. On comparing them, however, with those of the Dresden Codex, probably from this same quarter of the country, with those on the monument of Xochicalco, and with the ruder picture-writing of the Aztecs, it is not easy to discern any thing which indicates a common system. Still less obvious is the resemblance to the Egyptian characters, whose refined and delicate abbreviations approach almost to the simplicity of an alphabet. Yet the Palenque writing shows an advanced stage of the art, and, though somewhat clumsy, intimates, by the conventional and arbitrary forms of the hieroglyphics, that it was symbolical, and perhaps phonetic, in its character. That its mysterious import will ever be deciphered is scarcely to be expected. The language of the race who employed it, the race itself, is unknown. And it is not likely that another Rosetta stone will be found, with its trilingual inscription, to supply the means of comparison, and to guide the American Champollion in the path of discovery.

Brasseur de Bourbourg:
Histoire des nations civilisées du Mexique et de l'Amérique Centrale, durant les siècles antérieurs à Christophe Colomb
(Paris, 1857)

Up to that time I had not imagined for a moment that those beautiful regions had been inhabited, prior to the voyages of Christopher Columbus, by other men who were not savages. . . . Some time later I chanced to run across an edition of the *Journal des Savants* containing a summarized account of the report of Del Rio on the ruins of Palenque. It would be impossible for me today to describe the impression of astonishment mingled with pleasure that that account produced in me; and it was this that made me choose archaeology for my future vocation. A vague presentiment showed me, in the distance, mysterious veils that a secret instinct urged to lift; and hearing people speak of Champollion, whose fame was beginning to reach even the boarding schools in the provinces, I vaguely wondered whether the western continent as well might not contribute one day to the great scientific work being carried out in Europe.

Désiré Charnay and Viollette Leduc,
Cités et Ruines Américaines,
preface by Désiré Charnay (Paris, 1863)

The history and origin of those peoples offer a wide-ranging possibility for hypotheses. The first historians of that new world were not scholars. At that time, moreover, religion forbade investigations that were considered too erudite. Their descriptions, even those of the Conquistadors, were confined to banal comparisons with the cities of Spain, with a few Roman recollections thrown in here and there.

The traditions collected so far (without taking the Aztecs into consideration) have an apocryphal seal that must not escape the eye of the observer; it appears that biblical episodes, mixed in early times with ancient American legends, comes back to us in new versions, mingled with the poetic figures of those peoples, but still imbued with their sacred scent. . . . The Spaniards, in the days of the conquest, had every reason to get rid of the historical documents of the conquered peoples; they had to change them around at will, in good faith perhaps, judging the religions of their new subjects as abominations that had to be swept away and supplanted with the Catholic faith.

Jean Frédérick Waldeck,
Description des Ruines de Palenque
(Paris, 1866)

Descending to the west of the church of the village of Palenque, on a vast, rich grassy expanse, one sees on the right, at a distance of 1,100 feet, a high curious tree whose slender trunk rises up more than eight feet from ground level before spreading out its branches, which are themselves from thirty to forty feet high. The leaves of the tree are light green and are resplendent on the trunk, which is as smooth as that of the plane tree and the flowers grow in bunches of a lovely light yellow. I never before saw a tree like it, except only once, in the immense forest of the ruins. Precisely to the left of this rare, curious piece of vegetation begins the path that I cut out with the help of the compass and a chain, guided moreover by my valet, who was accustomed to passing through here on his way from the village to the ruins where every year he planted his plot of maize. . . . Having crossed the last creek, one climbs a steep slope with a 45-degree incline. This is where the ruins begin. A large number of squared stones are scattered all over the terrain, but the confusion is so great that it is difficult to determine exactly what type of building these stones were used for. There is reason to believe, however, that they formed one or more bastions of different heights aimed at blocking access to the city. Among other things one crosses a sixty-foot declivity so steep that a man on foot can barely manage it. In climbing, one hears the sound of a waterfall on the left, and, arriving at the top, discovers on the right the main building of the ruins, the Palace, which crowns a pyramid sixty feet high. If one starts out from the last house, east-northeast of the village, and continues south, crossing the Bajlunthie (River of Tigers), one comes upon two pyramids, three thousand five hundred steps from the point of departure, which I was the first to discover. I caught sight of them for the first time when I was seeking an isolated spot suitable for the growing of maize. The local inhabitants had no notion whatever of their existence, which was unknown even to Stephens.

Augustus Le Plongeon:
Sacred Mysteries Among the Mayas and the Quichés — Their Relation to the Sacred Mysteries of Egypt
(New York, 18—)

I will endeavor to show you that the ancient sacred mysteries, the origin of Free Masonry consequently, date back from a period far more remote than the most sanguine students of its history ever imagined. I will try to trace their origin, step by step, to this continent which we inhabit, — to America — from where Maya colonists transported their ancient religious rites and ceremonies, not only to the banks of the Nile, but to those of the Euphrates, and the shores of the Indian Ocean, not less than 11,500 years ago.

Anne Cary Maudslay and Alfred Percival Maudslay:
A Glimpse at Guatemala
(London, 1899)
Courtesy of John Murray (Publishers) Limited.

How can we assert that the Maya hieroglyphics were originated and developed within the Maya area until the ruins on the Rio Panuco, and at Teotihuacan, have been thoroughly excavated and explored, and up to the present they have only been scratched at? Did the development of Nahua culture affect that of the Mayas, and is that the reason why the art at Chichén has an indefinable Nahua flavour? We shall not know this for certain until the ruins in Tabasco, Campeche, and Petén have been thoroughly explored, and we can trace the connecting links. Amongst the many other puzzles, how are we to account for those curious mural paintings recently found by Dr. Gann in British Honduras, on the eastern limit of the Maya area, paintings essentially Nahua in style yet accompanied by a legend in Maya hieroglyphics? It is a fascinating subject for speculation, but the field offered for actual exploration is still more fascinating, and further research on the ground promises to supply facts worth more than volumes of dissertation built upon insufficient premises.

Within the Maya area there may, of course, have been many layers of culture widely removed in time which we cannot at present differentiate. Although it is not yet possible to trace the various stages which must have marked the evolution of the art which culminated in Copán and Palenque, it is not difficult to show that a great gap exists between the remains of those centres of ancient culture and the ruins of towns known to have been inhabited at the time of the Spanish invasion. I called attention to this fact when treating of the strongholds of the Quichés and Cachiquels, and have endeavoured in this chapter to show that the same gap yawns unbridged between Tayasal and Tikál. Prescott's picturesque account of the Astec city of Mexico, and Stephens's interesting description of the ruins he visited in Honduras, Tabasco, and Yucatán, aided by Fuentes's fabulous stories of the glories of Utatlan, have engendered a popular belief that at the time of the Spanish conquest the Indians throughout Central America were living sumptuously in magnificent stone-built cities. Such beliefs die hard, indeed they lay such hold of the imagination that from time to time enterprising newspapers echo the story told to Stephens sixty years ago by the Padre of Santa Cruz Quiché, and favour us with reports of Indian cities still inhabited and flourishing, hidden from the gaze of the vulgar by a wall of impenetrable forest.

Thomas Gann:
Ancient Cities and Modern Tribes
(London, 1926) Courtesy of Gerald
Duckworth & Co. Ltd.

We gave the animals their heads, for a mule's instinct is always to be trusted before a man's lack of intelligence, and were rewarded by the leading mule taking us straight to the ford down what had looked like a little cattle-track, from which even our topographical sense, shrivelled by the streets and numbers of civilisation, could not very well miss the road to the village.

Next day was almost perfect, a bright sun shining in a cloudless sky, the smoke from the burning pine-woods and corn plantations nearly completely cleared away by the rain of the previous night, and, better still, the ground so wet that it would be impossible for the Indians to set fire to the bush again for at least a couple of days.

Lindsay set out in the morning for the eastern hill-top stela, where he was joined by the rest of the party early in the afternoon.

About five the sun appeared, like a ball of red flame, in the western heavens, and as it neared the horizon gradually became dimmer and dimmer, till by the time it set over the hill-top it was absolutely invisible.

At 7.30 p.m. the great fire of split pine was set alight, as had been arranged by the men stationed on the western hill, and the illumination was so clear that the stela, directly behind which it stood, was clearly visible with glasses.

Lindsay has now obtained data which will make it possible to determine with absolute accuracy the day on which the sun, as viewed from the eastern marker, sets behind the western marker.

He has obtained the exact altitude of both the stelae above sea-level, with proper barometric corrections, the azimuth of the western from the eastern stela, and from Copán, azimuth of sunset from Copán, exact distance between the two stelae, by triangulation. He remained behind for further observations, but all these data must be submitted in the first place to the Department of Terrestrial Magnetism of the Carnegie Institution, of Washington.

The most remarkable discovery made, however, was the fact that the base of the eastern stela was on an exact level with the base of the western, which, in Lindsay's opinion, is a positive indication that the Maya were acquainted with some form of water-level.

The more we investigate the relics left by this remarkable people the more we realise that we have as yet merely scratched the surface of their knowledge in astronomy, physics, arithmetic, and art.

Reprinted with the permission of the
publisher from
The Ancient Maya, Third Edition
by Sylvanus Griswold Morley; revised
by George W. Brainerd (Stanford:
Stanford University Press, 1956) pp.
261–3.

Our best information on the living patterns of the Classic-stage Maya comes from the study of the domestic settlements near Uaxactún, which was carried out as follows: A large cross was laid out on the ground with its center at the main group of ruins, each arm being 400 yards wide and 1 mile long from the central point to its end. Each arm was divided into 68 squares, 100 yards to a side; each square contained 10,000 square yards, making a total of 272 squares for the four arms of the cross, or 2,720,000 square yards. It was thought that these squares would give a fair sample of the land in the immediate vicinity of the ceremonial and governmental center. Each square was examined carefully for traces of artificial construction, especially for vestiges of house sites, which would appear only as low mounds a foot or two above the ground level. The houses themselves, built of thatch and sapling, would have disappeared within a decade after the city was abandoned.

The survey showed that 43 per cent of the area examined was composed of logwood swamps or other uninhabitable terrain, leaving 57 per cent available for human occupation. Of this area, 400,000 square yards (14.7 per cent) were occupied by Groups A and E, the largest of the eight plaza-complexes at Uaxactún. This left a remainder of 1,140,000 square yards (114 squares) or about 42.3 per cent of the total area examined for domestic housing. These 114 squares contained 52 house mounds and 50 water reservoirs (*chultuns*), though no specific relationship between their locations could be ascertained.

Since the known occupation of Uaxactún lasted over a thousand years it seems likely that only a fraction of the house locations were occupied at one time. Although the normal Maya thatch house does not last more than about thirty years it is also probable that house mounds are often the result of several rebuildings of a house. Assuming occupancy of one out of eight houses, with five persons per house, gives a density of 136 persons per square mile. This density should be further lowered if it is taken into account that the normal Maya homestead consists of two or more houses and that about one-third of the house mounds near Uaxactún were in groups.

It is impossible to say how large an area was served by the religious and governmental center at Uaxactún, but it must be remembered that Tikal, the largest known Classic Maya center, is only ten miles away. This argues for a restricted drawing area for Uaxactún as well as an unusual density of population in the Uaxactún-Tikal region.

The problem of the population of the Maya lowland area may be attacked from an entirely different approach, that of the carrying capacity of the land. The modern state of Yucatán has an average population density of about 30 persons per square mile. Statistics over a recent ten-year period show that although a considerable percentage of the land is now planted to henequen, an export crop, the imports of corn amount to only about 2 per cent of the total required to sustain the native population, for whom this is still the chief staple.

If we accept a figure of 30 persons per square mile as the average carrying capacity over the whole lowland area — even with a possible error to half or double that density — we are faced with an amazing disparity between this area and a highland area such as the Valley of Mexico, where population density at the time of the Spanish Conquest is with some reliability estimated at about 500 per square mile. Theories that cultural advancement is proportional to population density are popular among present-day archaeologists, but do not easily explain the pre-eminence of the Classic Maya among New World cultures.

Charles Gallenkamp:
Maya: The Riddle and Rediscovery of a Lost Civilization
(New York, 1959) Courtesy of David McKay Company, Inc.

We have seen how the past century and a half brought Mayan archaeology forward from the limbo of skepticism and occult theorizing into the light of factual reconstruction and soundly based conjecture. Yet before archaeologists whose efforts have thus far revealed so much, there remains a vast sea of mystery. Many of the initial problems that confronted investigators of a century ago are still unresolved. Much remains to be learned concerning the evolution of Mayan civilization out of the Archaic horizon in Middle America. It is still not known exactly where in the pattern of early migrations the Mayoid tribes first assembled, or when, precisely, they settled in their tropical homeland. We can only hypothesize as to how and when the calendar and hieroglyphic writing made their appearance as dominating factors in Mayan development. Fully two thirds of their hieroglyphic script have yet to be deciphered and the presently meaningless inscriptions fitted into existing knowledge. There is virtually no information bearing upon the government of the city-states and their interrelationship in matters of trade and politics. Nor can we yet be certain of the conspiracy of events underlying the collapse of the Old Empire at the very height of its florescence. It remains an enigma without parallel in world history. Unlike the often-repeated rise and fall of modern and archaic empires — the recurrent theme of mankind's efforts to formulate an ideal state — Mayan civilization was started on its downward path by its own hand! Why? It is possible that we may never know.

A great deal concerning the Mexican period is still to be explained: the full story of the Itzás and the avenues by which they found their way into Yucatán, the source of the Quetzalcoatl-Kukulcán myth, and the entire intriguing panorama of petty lords and ruling dynasties whose conflicts left the Maya unprepared for the threat of Spanish invasion. . . .

When will it be that an explorer, a chicle gatherer, or perhaps a mining engineer will next stumble upon an astonishing discovery — new reflections of the genius that was the keynote of Mayan evolution; a guide by which the full range of glyphic writing can be deciphered; a graphic pictorialization of the events underlying the submission of the Old Empire — murals or hieroglyphic codices; unsuspected routes of trade with outside areas, or revelations concerning the identity of Kukulcán? Momentarily an accidental discovery might well clarify the riddle of centuries.

Immense portions of the ancient Mayan kingdom remain unexplored. The waters of the Usumacinta River flow past uncounted numbers of their desolate cities which no scientist has yet freed from jungle growth and the rubble of decay. In the Petén forest and the central reaches of the Yucatán Peninsula lie a myriad overgrown temples and shattered acropolises; and the mountainous highlands of Guatemala and Honduras are dotted with mounds and half-exposed structures.

Like Stephens, Maudslay, Thompson, and Ruz, other men will probe these unknown tracts until their secrets are finally reclaimed. The lure of such things is irresistible.

William R. Coe:
Tikal: A Handbook of the Maya Ruins
(1967)
Courtesy of the University Museum,
University of Pennsylvania.

Without the staggeringly difficult work of exploring and mapping all that lies about Tikal and without the unglamorous probing for what may lie in the otherwise blank areas spotted throughout central Tikal, there would be few grounds for estimating what the whole of ancient Tikal was like. Work such as this balances the other emphasis on temples, tombs, palaces, and monuments.

Reasonable questions as to how and why Tikal grew to what it became and what it really was in terms of social existence are not served by easy answers. Equally difficult to answer is why Tikal and all its Classic ramifications came to an end. This is really a matter of the collapse of lowland Maya civilization. Note has been made on the preceding pages of unfinished construction, such as the small abandoned temple in the West Plaza. Everything that is known points to a rapid disintegration of Classic authority and direction. What the actual causes were and why they had their effect when they did, about A.D. 900, are frankly unanswered by excavation. If archaeologists had a better grasp of what went on in Classic times — how people were organized among themselves and in relation to their environment — the seeds or preconditions of collapse might be better identified.

Chronological Chart of Middle American Civilization

YEAR —B.C.—	MAYA		MEXICO
3113	Beginning date of Maya chronology		Corn long cultivated; random settled farming
3000	ARCHAIC PERIOD	3000	
	Primitive farming life in Yucatán		Agriculture, villages, pottery spreading
1500	FORMATIVE (PRE-CLASSIC) PERIOD	1500	
	Early		
1200	Effective farming life spreading		Simple temple mounds being built
1000			
800	*Late*		Olmec culture growing in southern Mexico
	Maya-speaking peasantry established		
600	Tikal settled by this time		Cuicuilco pyramid destroyed
400			
300	*Protoclassic*		
200	Izapan influence on Mayan arts		Monte Alban culture emerging in Oaxaca
100			
A.D.		**A.D.**	
100			Pyramids of Sun & Moon built at Teotihuacán
200	292: lst datable inscription (Tikal)		
300	CLASSIC PERIOD	300	Teotihuacán influence spreading throughout Middle America
	Early		Veracruz culture thriving
400	Large ceremonial centers being built in Guatemala		
	460: First date at Copán		
500	Copán and Tikal thriving		Monte Albán culture thriving under Zapotecs
600	*Late*	600	
	633: First date at Palenque		Teotihuacán power declining
700			Mixtecs emerge as force in Oaxaca region
800			856: Tula founded
	879: Initial series at Chichén-Itzá		Zapotecs desert Monte Albán
	889: Last date and last classic stele		
900	POST-CLASSIC PERIOD	900	Toltecs dominating more of Middle America
	Collapse of classic Mayan culture in central Yucatán Metal-working introduced into Yucatán		Metal-working introduced into Mexico
1000	Toltecs from central Mexico move into Maya world; Chichén-Itzá developed by Toltec people		
1100			1160: Tula destroyed; small city-states emerge
1200	*Late*	1200	Proto-Aztec culture beginning
	Mayapán becomes "capital" of Yucatán		Mixtecs influential in Oaxaca region
1300	Bow and arrow introduced in Yucatán		
1400			1428: Aztecs emerge as power in central Mexico
	1461: Xiu people destroy Mayapán and impose rule; Yucatán split into rival city-states		
1500	1517: First Spaniards arrive at Tulúm	1500	1519: Cortés arrives in Mexico
	1542: Spanish established in Yucatán		1521: Cortés conquers Aztecs

Glossary

Actun: The Mayan term for both "cavern" and "temple."

Affix: A hieroglyphic group smaller than a principal sign (roughly half as large), which serves as a complement to the fundamental glyph.

Ahau: The last day of the twenty-day Mayan magical calendar month. It also means: "king," "emperor," "monarch," "prince," and "lord."

Ahaucan: Mayan term meaning "Lord Serpent" and designating the high priest.

Ah canul: ("the protectors"). A Mayan term used by the Mayapán leader Hunac Ceel as a sign of respect to designate his Mexican mercenaries.

Ah cuch caloob: A counselor to the supreme chief of a territory (halach uinic).

Ahkin: ("Lord-Sun"). A Mayan term used to designate the priests.

Ah leloob: The delegate chosen to help the governor (bataboob) collect the village tributes owed to the supreme chief of the territory.

Ah popol: The Mayan term designating the cantor in charge of dance and of musical instruments. He was also the head of the music house (popolna).

Ah Puch: The Mayan god of death.

Ah Xupan Xiu: The leader of Uxmal who headed the revolt against the Cocom dynasty at Mayapán in 1441.

Almehenoob: Mayan term designating the Yucatán nobility.

Atlatl: A Nahuan term for a typical Toltec weapon, a spear-and dart-throwing device that was small and flat with a groove in its center in which the dart was placed before being shot.

Atsbilán: ("He who sets the sun"). A name given to a statue in Yaxchilán by the Lacandón Indians, who believed it to be the head of a group of divinities who lived in the ruins of that city.

Aztecs: Indians of the Nahuan tongue who arrived in the central plateau of Mexico in the thirteenth century and dominated the country from the fifteenth century until the arrival of the Spanish.

Bacab: Four gods who were brothers and who escaped the floods that supposedly swallowed up the "three worlds" that existed before the Mayan one. Their duty was to hold up the sky from the four corners of the earth. They often assumed the aspect of a jaguar.

Baktun: A period of four hundred tun, or numerical years, of 360 days each.

Baktun 13: The name given by the Maya to the starting point of their chronological scheme, which (according to the Goodman-Martinez Hernandez-Thompson correlation) corresponds to 3113 B.C.

Bataboob: A Mayan word for the governors of the Yucatán before the Spanish Conquest.

Bolonkitu: The nine Mayan divinities of night and of the underworld.

Cakchiquel: An ethnic group from the mountainous region of Guatemala who spoke the Mayan language.

Can: Serpent.

Ce-acátl: The Nahuan designation for a phase of the Toltec calendar that means "One-Cane." It was one name of the Toltec king (Kukulkán) who founded Tula and Chichén-Itzá; and the term also designates Venus, the morning star.

Cenote: A natural well in the Yucatán that penetrates the limestone superstrata down to a stratum of underground water.

Chac: The Mayan god of rain.

Chaces: The assistants to the nacom (the priest responsible for human sacrifices) who held the victims during the ceremony (a Toltec-inspired custom).

Chacmool: ("Red Jaguar"). A term originally used improperly by the nineteenth century adventurer Augustus Le Plongeon to indicate a typically Toltec stone sculpture piece that represents a life-size man lying on his back with his chest raised on his elbows, his knees bent and his head turned towards the right. Although this term is inexact, it has been generally adopted.

Chakanputun: An ancient term for the Champoton volcanic agglomerate.

Champoton: The volcanic agglomerate at Tabasco in Mexico.

Chenes: (from the Mayan word chan: well). The central-southern region of the state of Campeche in Mexico, so named because of the numerous natural wells in this area. It has given its name to an architectural style in the Yucatán.

Chicle: The secretion of a sapodilla tree (Achras zapota) from which chewing gum derives.

Chiclero: A Spanish word designating the chicle harvester.

Chicomecoatl: ("seven serpents"). The Nahuan word used to designate an Aztec god.

Chilam: Diviner, soothsayer.

Chilam Balam, Books of: "The books of the occult soothsayers," according to Sylvanus G. Morley's translation. Indigenous manuscripts written in the Yucatán in the seventeenth and eighteenth centuries in the Mayan language but using Latin characters and set on paper. Each book is identifiable by the locality in which it was written. Ten or eleven fragments of these books are known, the most important of which are Chumayel, Mani, Tizimin.

Cóatl: Nahuan term used to indicate serpent.

Cocom: The reigning dynasty at Mayapán during its peak years.

Codex: In the Mayan civilization, an ancient hieroglyphic book containing multicolored painted signs on strips of vegetal fiber (bark) covered with a layer of slaked lime and folded many times (somewhat like an accordion).

Codex Dresden: One of the three remaining pre-Columbian Mayan codices, at present kept in the Dresden National Library. (Also called Codex Dresdensis.)

Codex Madrid: One of the three remaining original Mayan codices. (Also referred to as the Codex Tro-Cortesianus.)

Codex Nuttall: The pre-Columbian Mixtec codex now kept at the Oxford Bodleian Library.

Codex Paris: A pre-Columbian Mayan codex now kept at the Paris National Library. (Also referred to as the Codex Peresianus.)

Codex Vienna: A pre-Columbian Mixtec codex now kept at the Vienna National Library. (Also referred to as the Codex Vindobonensis.)

Count, Long: The term used to indicate the "initial series" Mayan method of dating, beginning from the chronological starting point (Baktun 13 — or 3113 B.C.) with the aid of a series of hieroglyphs.

Count, Short: A simplified method of Mayan dating, used in the Yucatán from the eleventh century on. It allowed for a margin of error of ten years in a 260 year cycle by using only the day Ahau accompanied by a cipher.

Copal: The resin of protium copal tree, which is used as an incense in Central America.

Cuautxicalli: The Nahuan word used to indicate the Aztec receptacle in which were deposited the hearts and blood of victims sacrificed to the gods.

Cumbu: The name of the eighteenth twenty-day month of the Mayan solar calendar.

Dating: end-of-period: The abbreviation for a Mayan "initial series," which makes it possible to write a date in three glyphs, with little risk of erring, over a range of 19,000 years.

Ehecatl: The Aztec god of wind, represented with a beak nose.

Glyph: The name sometimes given to the Mayan hieroglyph.

Glyphs, fundamental: The nucleus of calligraphic combinations in rectangular form; also called "principal signs."

Haab: The Mayan solar calendar containing 365 days.

Halach uinic: ("true man"). A Mayapán term designating the supreme chief of each territory in the Yucatán.

Hotun: Five numerical years, or the period of time equal to a fourth of a katun.

Hunab Ku: The great Mayan god, creator of the world and of all the Mayan divinities.

Hunac Ceel: A member of the Cocom dynasty who established the hegemony of Mayapán.

Imix: The first of the twenty days of the magical Mayan calendar month.

Itzá: The name of an ethnic group; later the name of the dynasty that ruled in Chichén-Itzá in the Yucatán.

Itzamná: The lord of the Mayan skies, son of Hunab Ku, and the inventor of writing.

Jade: A hard gem stone considered the most precious material in Central American civilizations. Jade played a fundamental role in art, religion, society, and magical practices in the pre-Columbian cultures. It was often an object of trade.

Kananka: The god of the forest of the indigenous Lacandón Indians.

Katun: The Mayan term for a period of twenty tun (or twenty years).

Kin: The sun, the day.

Kukul: The quetzal bird (Trogon splendens).

Kukulkán: The Mayan translation of the Nahuan term "Quetzalcoatl," or Plumed Serpent. Revered as a god by the Mayas.

Lacandón: The name of a group of Indians who speak Mayan and live in the Chiapas forests in Mexico near Yaxchilán and Bonampak. There are fewer than a hundred surviving today; they are the only Indians who have not undergone Christian or Spanish influence. They are considered the only authentic descendants of the classical period Maya.

Lahuntun: A period of time equal to a half katun, or ten numerical years (ten tun).

Macuilxochitl: ("Five flowers"). An Aztec god, patron of music and the arts.

Mani: A locality in the Yucatán where the Xiu dynasty went after the destruction of Mayapán.

Middle America: Indicates the cultural zone that includes Mexico, Guatemala, British Honduras and the western parts of El Salvador and Honduras.

Nacom: A Yucatán war chief who was elected every three years. This term also designated the priest in charge of human sacrifices.

Nahua: A northern population with elongated craniums and of great stature. There were many tribes in this category, among them the Toltecs, who infiltrated the central plateau of Mexico before the Aztecs. They spoke the Nahuan language.

Pentacoob: The name for slaves in the Yucatán.

Petén: ("isolated place"). The province composing the northern Guatemalan plains.

Pop: The name of the first of the eighteen twenty-day months in the Mayan solar calendar.

Popolna: The Yucatán meeting place where dance rehearsals were held and where musical instruments were housed.

Popol Vuh: "The Book of the Council," written in the sixteenth century in the Quiché-Mayan language with the help of Latin characters; it was found in the plateaus of Guatemala.

Puuc: The mountainous region of the Yucatán which gave its name to an artistic style of this peninsula.

Quetzal: The Nahuan term for the quetzal bird. It is the national emblem of Guatemala. In the pre-Columbian age its long tail feathers, a metallic greenish-blue, were reserved for the high priests and the sovereigns of Central America.

Quetzalcóatl: The "Plumed Serpent," in the Nahuan language. The name of a particular great king and the general honorary title of all Toltec priest-kings.

Río Bec: This important waterway, which runs along the Yucatán border, has given its name to an artistic style in the peninsula.

Roof comb: A tiled gable of perforated brickwork, which was built to decorate the top of a Mayan temple.

Sacbe: A Mayan road made of limestone covered with cement.

Stele: A sculptured monument of stone, usually an upright monolith.

Tabasco: A state in Mexico east of the Yucatán.

T'ao-T'ie: Chinese words of unknown origin which indicate a decorative motif present in the first bronzes of the Chinese Chang dynasty (1500 B.C.), a motif that appears to resemble the mask of the Mayan rain god Chac.

Tenayuca: Ancient capital of the Chichimechi, the Aztecs' ancestors, whose pyramid of five overlaid structures is surrounded by a sequence of serpents symbolizing the sun and fire.

Teotihuacán: Capital of the theocratic civilization bearing the same name that was developing by the outset of the Christian era in the central plateaus of Mexico. Forty miles from Mexico City, the site contains colossal pyramids of the moon and sun.

Tezcatlipoca: The Toltec god of war.

Tizimin: A village in the Yucatán where one book of *Chilam Balam* was found.

Tlaloc: The Nahuan god of rain; one of the oldest gods in the central plateau of Mexico.

Tlapallan: "The Land of the Aurora," in the Nahuan tongue.

Toltecs: The designation for all the tribes that moved to the central plateau of Mexico at the end of the eighth century. The Toltecs destroyed Teotihuacán and were the founders of Tollan (Tula). They ruled the Mayan people of the Yucatán for a period of time, as indicated by evidence found on several Mayan sites.

Tula (Tollan): The Toltec capital (in modern Mexican state of Hidalgo).

Tun: Indicating, in Mayan, the 360-day period used in the calculation of time; a numerical year.

Tzompantli: "The Wall of Skulls," in Nahuan. This is a rectangular platform used to support a type of fence on which were placed the heads of sacrifice victims.

Uayeb: Name of the nineteenth and last month of the "solar year." This was the unusual month that had five days instead of twenty. It means, in Mayan, "that which has no name."

Uinal: A period of twenty *kin*, or twenty days.

Xaman Ek: The Mayan god of the polar star.

Xibalbá: ("under region"). A locality mentioned in the *Popol Vuh* and inhabited by the "Owls," supposedly perverse men and enemies of humanity.

Xiu: The dynasty that reigned in Uxmal during its peak years.

Yucatán: The peninsula of Mexico in Central America and including its easternmost state of the same name.

Yum Kax: The Mayan god of maize.

Zamna: An early Mayan god; possibly the origin of the word *Maya* for the people themselves.

Recommended Reading

There are many books about the various aspects of the Maya; the problem is to find the ones best suited to a reader's particular level and needs. This list is merely a selection of books that complement various aspects touched on by this volume. They have also been chosen on the basis of accessibility — their price, their recent printings, and their attempts to communicate with the general public.

Benson, Elizabeth P.: *The Maya World.* Crowell (New York, 1967)

Bernal, Ignacio: *3000 Years of Art and Life in Mexico.* Abrams (New York, 1969)

Book of Chilam Balam of Chumayel: trans. by Ralph L. Roys. Univ. of Oklahoma Press (Norman, 1967)

Coe, Michael: *The Maya.* Praeger (New York, 1966); Thames & Hudson (London, 1966)

Covarrubias, Miguel: *Indian Art of Mexico and Central America.* Knopf (New York, 1957)

Landa, Diego de: *Relación de las Cosas de Yucatán,* trans. & ed. by Alfred M. Tozzer. Peabody Museum (Cambridge, 1941)

Leon-Portilla, Miguel: *Pre-Columbian Literatures of Mexico.* Univ. of Oklahoma (Norman, 1969)

Morley, Sylvanus G.: *The Ancient Maya.* Stanford Univ. Press (Stanford, 1956: 3rd ed. rev. by Brainerd)

Peissel, Michel: *The Lost World of Quintana Roo.* Dutton (New York, 1963); Hodder (London, 1964)

Popol Vuh, The Sacred Book of the Ancient Quiché Maya: trans. by Goetz and Morley. Univ. of Oklahoma (Norman, 1950)

Proskouriakoff, Tatiana: *Album of Maya Architecture.* Univ. of Oklahoma (Norman, 1963)

Thompson, J. Eric S.: *Maya Archaeologist.* Univ. of Oklahoma (Norman, 1963) *The Rise and Fall of Maya Civilization.* Univ. of Oklahoma (Norman, 1966, 2nd ed.) with Merle Greene: *Ancient Maya Relief Sculptures.* N.Y. Graphic Society (Greenwich, 1967)

Wauchope, Robert: *They Found the Buried Cities.* Univ. of Chicago (Chicago, 1965)

West, Robert; Wauchope, Robert; Willey, Gordon; Ekholm, Gordon; *et al.: Handbook of Middle American Indians,* 9 vols. Univ. of Texas (Austin, 1964–70)

Wolf, Eric: *Sons of the Shaking Earth.* Univ. of Chicago (Chicago, 1959)

Recommended Viewing

Nothing makes the world of the Maya seem so real as a visit to the actual sites. Using such cities as Mérida, in Mexico's State of Yucatán, or Guatemala City as bases, you can visit many of the principal sites; details about such trips can be obtained from governmental tourist bureaus or private travel agencies.

The next best thing is a visit to a museum with a collection of Mayan artifacts or cultural displays. The world's finest collections of Mayan works are in the National Museum of Anthropology in Mexico City and the National Museum in Guatemala City, but there are also fine collections in the following museums:

GREAT BRITAIN
> Birmingham City Museum and Art Gallery, Birmingham
> The British Museum, London
> The Victoria and Albert Museum, London

U.S.A.: New York City
> The American Museum of Natural History
> The Museum of Primitive Art
> The Metropolitan Museum of Art
> The Museum of the American Indian, Heye Foundation
> The Brooklyn Museum

In addition, there are many other collections throughout the United States — all open, within certain restrictions, to the general public. The list below includes the major collections that offer people everywhere a chance to star an acquaintance with the remains of this extraordinary people.

Arizona: †Phoenix: Heard Museum of Anthropology and Primitive Art
> †Tucson: Arizona State Museum
California: †Berkeley: Lowie Museum of Anthropology, University of California
> *Los Angeles County Museum of History, Science and Art
Colorado: †Denver Museum of Natural History
Connecticut: †New Haven: Yale University Art Gallery
District of Columbia (Washington): †The U.S. National Museum. *The Dumbarton Oaks Research Library and Collection
Illinois: †Chicago Natural History Museum
> †Chicago Art Institute
Louisiana: *New Orleans: Middle American Research Institute, Tulane University
Massachusetts: *Cambridge: Peabody Museum of Archaeology and Ethnology
Minnesota: †Minneapolis Institute of Arts
Missouri: †Kansas City: William R. Nelson Gallery of Art
New Mexico: †Albuquerque: Museum of Anthropology
Ohio: †Cleveland Museum of Art
Pennsylvania: *Philadelphia: University Museum, University of Pennsylvania
> †Pittsburgh: Carnegie Museum
Rhode Island: †Providence: Rhode Island School of Design, Museum of Art
Wisconsin: †Milwaukee Public Museum

* = especially rich in Maya materials
† = some Maya among Middle American materials

INDEX

Numbers in italics indicates illustrations.